The Nichols Connection

to Ancient and Royal Families

Ancestry, A to Z

Helen Brown Nichols

HERITAGE BOOKS
2007

HERITAGE BOOKS
AN IMPRINT OF HERITAGE BOOKS, INC.

Books, CDs, and more—Worldwide

For our listing of thousands of titles see our website
at
www.HeritageBooks.com

Published 2007 by
HERITAGE BOOKS, INC.
Publishing Division
65 East Main Street
Westminster, Maryland 21157-5026

International Standard Book Number: 978-0-7884-3364-1

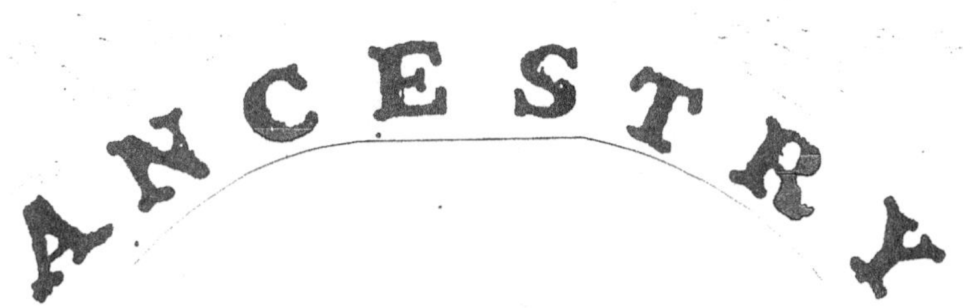

Leo Nichols

and

Helen Lee Fern Brown

by

Helen Brown Nichols

Dedication

Almost forty years have come and gone since I started ancestor hunting. Research continues still. Family is number one, and with the love of my family, genealogical research is the way of life. The results have been rewarding. The information I've collected is still growing, and is such, that the need to do something with it has been long overdue. The *Nichols* is the beginning of several books planned. Our ancestry included so many different surnames that the title "*A to Z Ancestry of Leo Nichols and Helen Lee Fern Brown*" is just that... A to Z. I'm so thankful for all the help and encouragement I've received from so many. I can not thank each of you enough. Building up memories with you, has made my life worth living.

A Note from Me.... Janie Nichols Boyd

This book is in the *present order* with the *reader* in mind. I feel that the *reader* can best understand how the *Nichols* connections were formed. Some of the pages are repeated ones, so the reader can "connect the dots" so to speak. Although my eyes have seen these pages many times over, please forgive any errors that I may have overlooked. English was never my strong suit!

Brian Day, thank you for all your help and patience. Without your computer knowledge, I would not have made it this far.

To my children Jonathan, JaLynn, and Robert, thank you for all your help and interests.

Michael Martin, thank you for the use of your computer!

I would like all to know that was my pleasure to help my mom finally have this book come to a *reality*, when I know it has been one of her dreams for so long. Thanks to mom and her research, we now know of, and about, our Nichols lineage. Years of her "work of love" will always be part of our history, and will be carried on for generations to come. I think I can speak for all of us when I say, " thank you mom."

Love, Janie

CONTENTS

The Nichols Connection

A Little Something About This Book

This is about my new book, **The Nichols Connection**. What is it? Connection to what? You may ask these and other questions. Let me try to tell you about my book. It is a one of a kind, an original, **Nichols** book. It is packed with information, easy to see how one ancestor links to the others.

When I told my granddaughter I'd like to write about each ancestor, she suggested I put a pedigree chart above my story, so the reader could easily tell how the person is related to the reader. Other suggestions were given by several loved ones. An attempt has been made to provide an interesting "who begot who" lineage from generations 1. to the top of the charts. By starting with the first step and climbing up the family tree, ancestor by ancestor, the reader will come to know each of them. Then, when the ancient ancestor appears, a better understanding will be possible.

When my father told me about his ancestors of long ago, I was in disbelief about some of the more famous ones. That is until I came to know them. Know them? Yes! I feel I know them well. Now I understand how proud my father was of his family. You will be proud too. You certainly have an ancestry that will make you proud! My book does not begin with the oldest known ancestor. It does begin with my husband, **Leo Nichols**. My husband is the grandson of **Joseph A. B. Nichols** and **Martha Jane Cannon**. **Joseph** and **Martha** had four children whose names were:

William Daniel Nichols
Thomas Jefferson Nichols
Alabama Nichols
Martin Van Buren Nichols

They are better known as **Will, Tom, Dolly**, and **Dock**. The annual **Nichols** reunion is given in their honor.

This book is about their ancestry and descendants. Of course other genealogical data is included. There are charts, pedigrees, and information obtained from *actual* records (marriages,wills, deeds, etc..) when it was made available. The Civil War data of **Willis W. Nichols** will be useful for one wanting to be a *Son* or a *Daughter of the Confederacy*. To be a *Son* or a *Daughter of the American Revolution*, there is helpful information available. When my daughter submitted a D.A.R. application on **Churchill Blakey** as the Revolutioinary War Patriot, the information she submitted proved the connection beyond a reasonable doubt.

There are other organizations for which you are eligible. There is no possibility of this being a complete ancestry. I regret it is not possible for me to compile all the information I've gathered during my lifetime. If this book sparks your interest and causes you to go ancestor hunting, then all my efforts will have been worthwhile.

With very best wishes,

Helen Brown Nichols

More Than A Name

There are many stories behind the names on the charts. The names are representatives of people with a life, and a life is a story within itself. Whatever their position in life, (Kings or Queens, Cardinals, Inventors, Explorers, servants, or political outcasts), their true stories have been documented and are about to be unraveled, to show, they are *more than a name*.

NICHOLS

PEDIGREE CHART

numbers indicate generation of descent

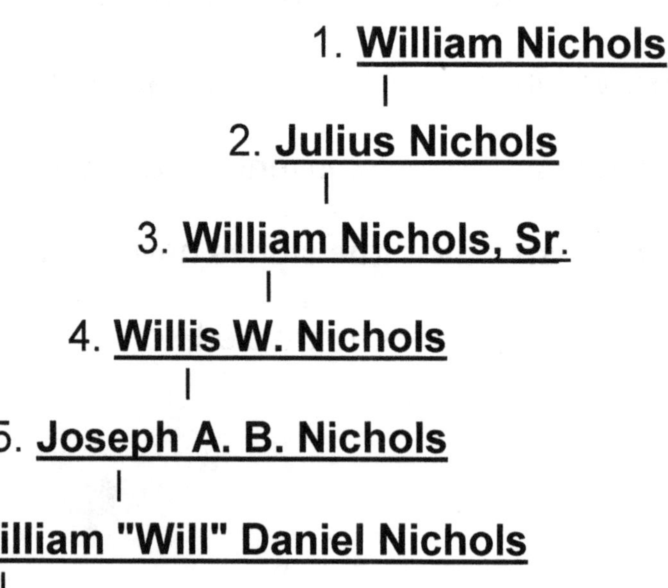

(1.) Will, 2 June 1772, Bute Co. N. C. (2.) Will, 23 Jan. 1803, Abbeyville District S.C. (3) 1790-1850 (4.) S.C.-Tx. (5.) Tx.-Tx. (6.) Tx.-La.) (7.) La.

The Nichols's Signatures And Pedigree Chart

(Will 2 June 1772
Bute Co. N.C.)

WILLIAM NICHOLS 1772

Julius Nichols 1803

Wm Nichols

WILLIAM NICHOLS 1837

W. W. Nichols

Willis W. Nichols 1874

JOSEPH A.B. NICHOLS 1874

W N Nichols 1905

(WILL)

Leo Nichols

LEO NICHOLS 2001

Leo Nichols

Signatures & Dates signed.

Leo & Helen

Leo Nichols

Leo Nichols **married** **Helen Lee Fern Brown**
Colfax, Grant Parish, La.
Dec. 23, 1950

children

Ronnie Edmund

Barbara Ann

Carolyn Faye

Belinda Lanae

Leo Stephen

Daniel Norman

Janie Lucretia

Carolyn
Belinda
Daniel
Janie
Barbara
Ronald
Stephen

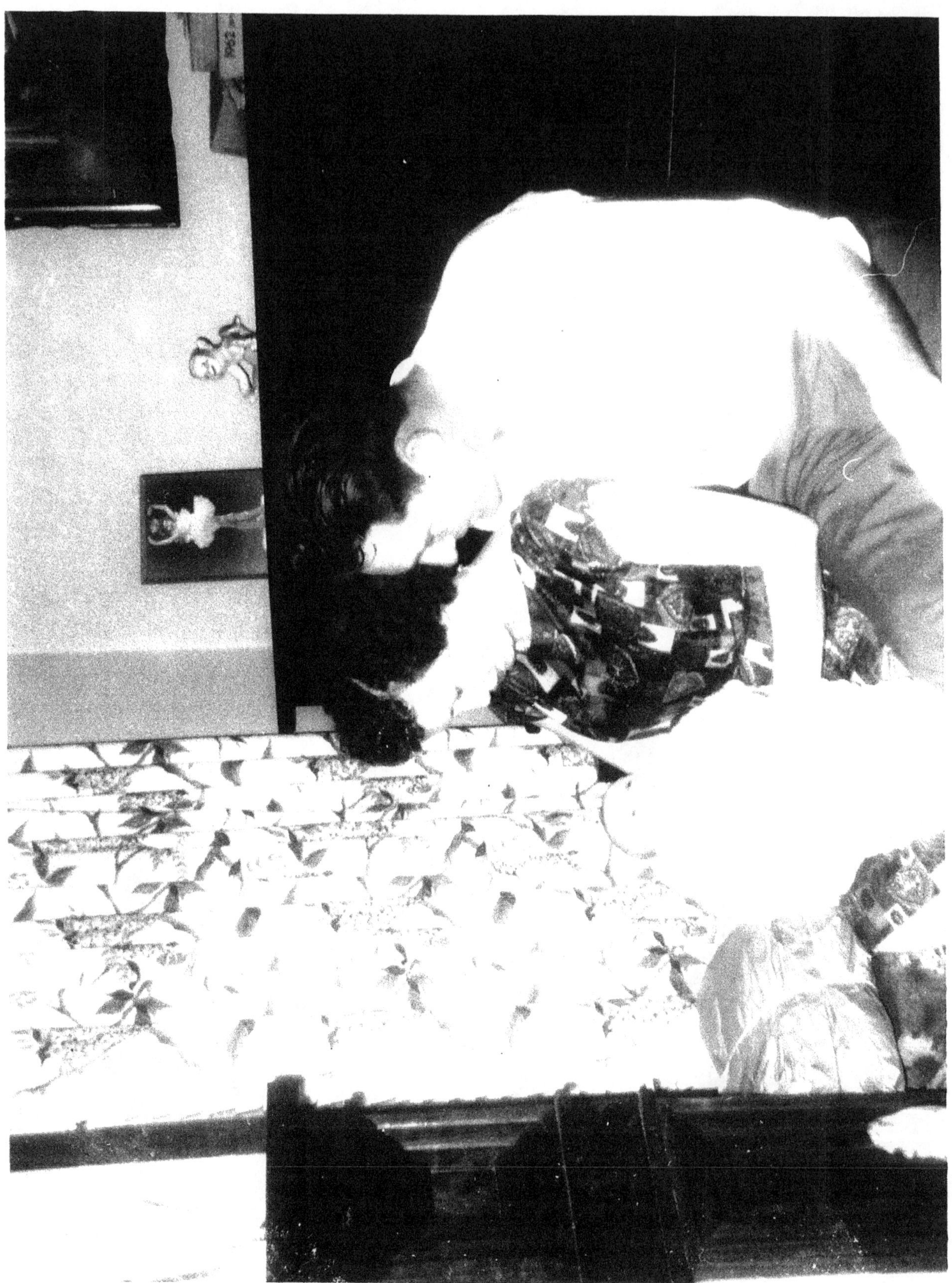

A VETERAN'S HERO

"I wouldn't be here if it wasn't for you", Ronnie told his father. "What you taught me on those hunting and camping trips is the reason I'm alive today. I owe my life to you, Daddy"

By the age of eight, Ronnie had his own hunting rifle and shotgun. I wish I could remember just what age he was that first time his father took him hunting.

When Ronnie "opens up" and talks about the experiences he had (as a United states Marine Corp. scout sniper in Viet Nam), and refers to "What and How" his father taught him helped him to survive and confirms that Ronnies hero is his father Leo Nichols.

Ronnie's Mother
Helen Brown Nichols

Get That Sporting
You've Always Wanted

A VETERAN'S HERO

"I wouldn't be here if it wasn't for you", Ronnie told his father. "What you taught me on those hunting and camping trips is the reason I'm alive today. I owe my life to you, Daddy"

By the age of eight, Ronnie had his own hunting rifle and shotgun. I wish I could remember just what age he was that first time his father took him hunting.

When Ronnie "opens up" and talks about the experiences he had (as a United states Marine Corp. scout sniper in Viet Nam), and refers to "What and How" his father taught him helped him to survive and confirms that Ronnies hero is his father Leo Nichols.

Ronnie's Mother
Helen Brown Nichols

Our Heroes

History gives a good picture of how our ancestors built and defended our country. The kind of history they made could never be repeated. They fought before the Battle of Point Pleasant, 1774, and the "2nd Battle of Point Pleasant",1778, at Fort Donnally.

Our heroes were on the homefront as well as on the battlefield. Their uniform was white, of colors, and everyday dress. True in the past and in the present. Too many go to war. Too many lives given. Still, we have the horror of war. We hold together and strong. We are Americans. God Bless America and all who serve.

Ronald Edmund Nichols

Viet Nam

NICHOLS
U.S.
U.S.
29
NICHOLS
CAROLYN
FAYE

Cleo Nichols

Korean War

K.C. Nichols

World War II

J.R. Nichols

World War II

Leo Nichols Father

Will Nichols

Overseer of plantation

working

German World War II prisoners

Leo's Parents

Leo's twin brother Cleo
and their father

William Daniel Nichols (Will)

The oldest of four children, Will Nichols was born in Texas. His full name is William Daniel Nichols. His father, Joseph A.B. Nichols, died when Will was twelve years of age. His mother, Martha Jane Cannon Nichols, and his stepfather, R. J. Methvin, married in Rapides Parish, La. Will Nichols worked on their farm until he married and homestead property of his own. By 1910, he had been married twice, was on the Rapides parish, La. census, widowed, with five living children. He married a third time to Lillian Coutee Basco, who was also widowed in 1910. She had children. Will and Lillie Nichols were parents of eleven children. Their twin sons, Cleo and Leo, were the youngest boys, and Annie Nichols was their youngest child. My father-in-law died in 1955, at home on the plantation where he has lived, near Boyce, La. An Annual Nichols family reunion began in 1956. My mother-in-law was present. My husband, Leo, has attended all forty-five that has been held, in honor of his father Will Nichols, and all the children of Joseph A. B. Nichols.

William Daniel Nichols
(Will, W.D., W.N.)

W.D. **married** Rosa Brellan
children: Mattie, Bud, Ollie, and Dock

W.N. **married** Josephine Rachal
children: Rosa Lee, Carrie, and two infants

William **married** Lillie Coutee
children: Edna Mae, Willie, Joe, Lillie Mae, Janie, K.B., K.C, J.R., Cleo, Leo, and Annie
(Cleo and Leo are twins)

Lillie Coutee **married** first to Cleveland Basco (1887-1910)
children: Cleveland A. (known as Ed Mirse) and Maggie

Leo Nichols Father

William Daniel "Will" Nichols

(son of **Joseph A. B. Nichols** and
Martha Jane Cannon Nichols)

all his children

Mattie, Bud, Ollie, Dock, Rosa Lee, Carrie, Edna Mae, Willie, Joe, Lillie Mae, Janie, K.B., K.C., J.R., (twins Cleo and Leo), Annie
*Ed Basco, *Maggie Basco

*please see page 8

Joseph A.B. Nichols

married

Martha Jane Cannon

Jan.15,1874

children

William Daniel
(known as **Will**)

Thomas Jefferson
(known as **Tom**)

Alabama
(known as **Dolly**)

Martin Van Buran
(known as **Dock**)

Martha Jane Cannon Nichols married 2nd to Redding Jasper Methvin (R.J.) on Dec.27, 1887

Joseph A. B. Nichols

Joseph A. B. Nichols was the son of Willis W. Nichols and his second wife Elizabeth Clark Blakey. He was born near Nacogdoches at Melrose, 1851, in Nacogdoches County, Texas. He was a "traveling medicine man, what they called a drummer," I was told about 40 years ago. It seemed no one could give me more information about my husband's grandfather except his name was maybe "Joe or Joseph" and he died when children were young. I was told "No, you won't be able to find him." But I did find him and more. His marriage record really gave me encouragement and exciting data to add to my genealogical research. In part, it read "Mr. Joseph Nichols and Miss Martha J. Cannon at the residence of the Bride's mother in Sabina Parish and in presence of the undersigned witnesses, January the 15th 1874." Both signatures, Joseph Nichols and Martha J. Cannon, plus the signature of W. W. Nichols, was on the marriage certificate. Joseph's father was one of the witnesses. More records were found and research continues still. It seems so little is known about this man, but this man "Joe or Joseph" did make a difference. His full name is Joseph Anthony Blakey Nichols, named for his grandfather, Joseph Anthony Blakey. His ancestry is one all hope to find in their family tree.

The interest continues to grow with each find and documentation. Joseph's tie to this worthy ancestry is though his mother, Elizabeth Clark Blakey, second wife of Willis W. Nichols, who was a widower with three children. Joseph's mother, Elizabeth Clark Blakey Nichols, was the mother of seven children. When about 36, Joseph died leaving a widow and four children. These children are

known by the names *Will, Tom, Dolly*, and *Dock Nichols*. 12
They are connected to a dream come true ancestry, through their father, Joseph Anthony Blakey Nichols, (Joe or Joseph) who did, indeed, make a difference.

1147

The State of Louisiana Parish of Sabine.
This is to certify that in obedience to a marriage licence isued by the Clerk the Dist Court in said Parish and to me directed I have this day celebrated the rites of matrimony between Mr Joseph Nichols and Miss Martha J.Cannon at the residence of the Brides Mothers in Sabine Parishard in the presence of the undersigned witnesses January the 15th 1874.
Witnesses:
Clint Arthur
W.R.Curtis — Joseph Nichols.
W.W.Nichols — Edmund Duggen Minister of the Gospel — Martha J.Cannon
Filed January ~~9~~ 19th 1874
R.W.Sibley Clerk
Recorded September 5th 1925.

"

1148

State of Louisiana Parish of Sabine. Act of Marriage.
Be it remembered that on the 9 day of Janary A. D. 1894, Hudson Broach and Mary Nobles Boath residents of the Parish of Sabine personally came before me H.H.Calins Justiceof the Peace in and for the Parish Sabine together with the undersigned witnesses of full age and residents inthe said Parish and that then and there the said Hudson Broach and Mary Nobles having produced the Licence required by law signified desire and intention before us the said Justice and witnesses to be united in the estate of matrimony whereupon after due proclamation made and no impediment being suggested they the said Hubon Broach and Mary Nobles were by me the said Justice in the presence of the said witnesses joined wed lock according to the laws of State of Louisiana and duly pronounced to be Husband and wife.
In testimony whereof the parties to the said marriage affix their signature to with the said Justice and witnesses.
Attest: his
Spence X [illegible]
mark. — his Hudson X Broach mark.
his
Henry X Nobles, — her Mary X Nobles mark.
mark.
H.H.Calins J.P. 7 Ward.
Filed February 28th 1874.
R.W.Sibley Clerk Court.
Recorded Sept 5th1925.

Thomas Jefferson "Tom" Nichols 13

(son of **Joseph A.B. Nichols** and **Martha Jane Cannon Nichols**)

children

Ida Gertrude
Lucy Ella
Tommy Jefferson
Eddie E.
Johnnie Walker
Maud Etdel
William Lawrence
DeWitte D'quin
Laura Rilla
Effie Elizabeth

Alabama "Dolly" Nichols

(**daughter of Joseph A.B. Nichols and Martha Jane Cannon Nichols**)

children

Joseph
Bubbie Jefferson
Willis Van Buran
Alfred Ellis
Ada Latticia
Woodrow Wilson

Martin Van Buran "Dock" Nichols

(son of Joseph A.B. Nichols and Martha Jane Cannon Nichols)

children

Maybella
Milton
Melvin
Katie
Alice
Tiny Elizabeth
Robert
Irene
William Bell

The Nichols Connection to Ancient and Royal Families

Leo Nichols Great Grandfather

*** WILLIS W. NICHOLS ***

married 1844

6. ELIZABETH CLARK BLAKEY

I I I

1st Elizabeth James
children
Daniel Milton
William M.
Martha J.

children
Susan M.
Alabama D.
Fanny O. (twin)
Candis G. (twin)
Joseph A.B.
John W.
Georgia A.W.

3rd Mary Ann ___
children

I

Ancestry of

I

10. PENELOPE JOHNSON

++++++++++++++++++++++

wife of

CAPTAIN CHRISTOPHER CLARK

Willis W. Nichols

Willis W. Nichols and his parents were born in South Carolina. They were on the 1840 census of Bibb County, Ala. where Willis W. Nichols married twice. Both wives were named Elizabeth. The first was Elizabeth James, who died young, leaving her husband and three children. The second was Elizabeth Clark Blakey, daughter of Joseph Anthony Blakey. They were parents of seven children, one of which, was Joseph A. B. Nichols, born 1851, at Melrose, Nacogdoches County Texas. His parents were on the 1850-1860 census, but the 1870 census of Nacogdoches County shows Joseph living with his father and his third wife, Mary Ann. According to the records found on Willis W. Nichols, he was an active, knowledgeable man of apparent great strength and courage. He was a land owner, Justice of the Peace, and served in the Civil War. He was also a Texas Ranger.

Name & Rank: Nichols, W. W., 1st Sgt.
Comm. Off: Eubank, Elias N., Capt.
Organ: Co.B Inf., Nacogdoches Co., 3rd Brig., TST
Enlist: S.19-63 at Camp Simpson for 6 months

Disch:
Descrip: Age 49 (on roll dtd. Mar.15-64)

Remarks: R&F 147; En.Off. F.B.Sublett; 1st org. listed as above; on Jy 16-63 Co.B Inf. for Angelina & Nacogdoches Co., 3rd Brig. by order Maj.Gen.Magruder tr.to CSA to serve for 6 months; on Mar.15-64 Capt.

(Over)

Eubank's Co., now Co.C, 2nd Regt.Inf., 3rd Brig., reörganized at Camp Simpson under Act D.15-63; 3 MR, 1 dtd. Jan.26-63, 1 dtd. Jy 16-63 & 1 dtd. Mar.15-64. Name only on roll dtd. Mar.15-64.

Justice of the Peace

Willis W. Nichols gave Oath, Justice of the Peace of Nacogdoches County,Texas, on 17 Aug. 1852, 11 Aug. 1864, and 28 Feb. 1866.

From **Marriage Records of Nacogdoches County, Texas**, page 136 by Mrs. R Q Murrie.

Willis W. Nichols on list of qualified Jurors:

	page
no. 242 July 5, 1858	4
no. 231 July 2, 1866	69
no. 10 Jan. 18, 1866	73
no. 294 July 7, 1862	39
no. 261 ---------	47
no. 947 ---------	106

Data from book Lis Pendens at Nacogdoches County Courthouse, Nacogdoches Texas.

Willis W. Nichols

Willis W. Nichols owned land in Sabine Parish, La. and was on tax delinquent list.

Tax Delinquet Book I

$84.20 and with 8% interest to 1874

Assessed 1.90
amount. tax 2.75

Copy of note made from research at Many, La. Courthouse (Sabine Parish)

Our Willis W. Nichols was born *1816* in *South Carolina*. He married three times. On the 1870 census of Nacogdoches County, Texas, he was with third wife Mary Ann _____. The 1880 census of Hopkins County, Texas showed a Willis Nichols and Mary A. E. He was from Mississippi. The date of death for Willis W. Nichols, father of Joseph A. B. Nichols, remained unknown. He was witness 1874 to his son's wedding. He probably died in Nacogdoches County, Texas.

- Not Our Willis-

Willis	Mary Ann
Jan. 6, 1831	Sept. 10, 1840
Jan. 10, 1884	April 15, 1885

In Como Cemetery at Hopkins County, Texas

Eizabeth James Nichols
James burial plot
Centervillle Memorial Community Cemetery
in Bibb County, Alabama

Elizabeth James Nichols was the first wife of Willis W. Nichols. They were married on August 11, 1836 in Bibb County, Alabama. They were parents of Daniel Milton, William M. and Martha J. Nichols. Elizabeth died young. She was buried in the James burial plot in Centreville, Alabama. She had a gravestone with the inscription:

Sacred to the memory of Elizabeth Nichols,
who was born April 14th 1822
and departed this life July 5th 1854
Aged 32 years, 2 months, and 21 days

Elizabeth James Nichols was the daughter of Frederick and Martha James. The following data was copied. Sacred to the memory of Martha James, wife of Frederick James who was born July 26th 1802 and departed this life April 25th 1843, aged 40 years, 8 months, and 29 days. Frederick James, born in Pitt County, North Carolina, March 31, 1793 having no other dates. Frederick James was Justice of the Peace of Bibb County. He left a Will dated the 25th of May in 1863. A wife, Sarah Jane James was mentioned including children and property with slaves. There is a Milton Nichols buried there also. His name is inscribed on a double C. S. A. marker, with Pleasant W. James. The death date is February 3, 1862 for both of them. Pleasant W. James was born April 23, 1843. The Birthdate of Milton Nichols was not inscribed.

Neighbors

Frederick James	Jane Nichols
children	**children**
Sarah	Joseline G.
Clarborn	William M.
John C.	Sarah G.
Columbus F.	Julius
Mariah E.	
William E.D.	

1850 Census of Bibb County, Alabama
19 September 1850

Frederick James was the father of Elizabeth James, first wife of **Willis W. Nichols**, and the grandfather of their three children.

Elizabeth G. James, wife of Samuel Martin, died at age 26. She was native of Botetourt County, Virginia, and daughter of Frederick W. James and Dorothy Ann (Dandridge, descendant of Pocohontas?) Elizabeth G. James (Mrs. Samuel Martin, merchant) moved to Madison Co. Ala., then in 1836 to Macon, Miss. See Alabama Records, Dandrud Vol. 12 p. 79 for more information.

A neighbor of William Nichols, Sr. and Jane Nichols, parents of Willis W. Nichols, was a Frederick James, born c 1795 may possibly be son of Frederick W. James (died 1824 Madison Co. Ala.) and Dorothy Ann Dandridge. Both William Nichols, Sr. and Frederick James lived west of the Cahaba River in Bibb Co. Ala. Frederick James was Justice of the Peace. His daughter Elizabeth James married Willis W. Nichols and they had three children. Any blood relations of the older Nichols and James families is not known, but they may have traveled together (?) from Virginia to North and South Carolina before becoming next door neighbors near Centreville in Bibb Co. Alabama.

Succession of

Thomas Constable

Leo Nichols great grandmother, Mary Ann _?_ was the mother of Martha Jane Cannon. Mary Ann _?_ first marriage was to Daniel C. Cannon, and her second husband was Thomas Constable. The Succession of Thomas Constable names his, hers, and their minor children.

Fannie O. Nichols

(Leo Nichols great Aunt)

married 1st

John Sylvester Nichols

children

James A
Laura

married 2nd

Wylie Terrell

children

John
Martha (twin)
Mary (twin)
Nute
Eligiah
Frances
Liddya
Jane
Wyllie Pleasant

Fannie O. Nichols was a sister of Joseph A.B. Nichols.

Georgia Ann W. Nichols

married

James Lewis McBride

children

John William
Henry J.
Fannie Elizabeth

Georgia Ann W. Nichols, (Leo Nichols great Aunt) was a sister of **Joseph A. B. Nichols**.

Alabama Nichols

married

Joseph W. Rector
11 June 1868

children

Florence E.

The parents of **Alabama Nichols** Rector were Willis W. Nichols and Elizabeth Clark Blakey. Alabama had a niece named Alabama, only daughter of Joseph A. B. Nichols, and called "Dolly".

Alabama Nichols was a sister of Joseph A. B. Nichols.

(Leo Nichols Great Aunt)

The Days that Lie Behind Us

Tis not for Hope, the starry eyed, to think of days behind us;
Tis not for Joy to stem the tide, and of the Past remind us;
But Memory loves to think of them, those bygone hours to cherish;
She wears them all, a Diadem whose beauty ne' er shall perish!

And often when the twilight hou O'er hill and valley's falling,
A Voice of sweetness and of power seems to our spirits calling;
Then Fancy comes from realms of bliss, with wondrous Charm to
bind us,
And memory turns and wafts a kiss to days that lie behind us!

Today may be the watchword still the call to strong endeavor
Tomorrow from the future's hill may beckon us forever;
But far away down memory's stream the twilight hour shall find us;
There would we drift awhile and dream of days that lie behind us.

T. Russell Shelton
Published in the *Times Dispatch*
11 January 1904 Richmond, Virginia

Back to Cemetery Hunting

My friend Gloria and I have gone to many places together, looking for our ancestors over the years. We have gone to libraries, archives, courthouses, churches, funeral homes, businesses, the homes of authors, historians, and have had personal interviews, and many others. We wanted to find our people, and find out all we could about them. Our trips took us to old home places, rivers, and back roads. No matter where we travel, we managed to do some cemetery hunting. It didn't matter where. There was always something different to find. In one cemetery, a large bell on a pedestal, the largest I've ever seen, was near the church. We found out it was the "town bell" and it was a way to tell people news, once they heard the bell ring and gathered there. Also found out the land was donated to the Methodist Church by Walter Reid, my ancestor. We can never tell what we might find in genealogy. Sometimes what we find is not what we believe it to be. Now I'm one of those that want to know for sure that who I've found is really him or her.

Let me go back to the cemetery hunting part of my story. In Hopkins County, Texas, Gloria and I went to the Como Cemetery. I remember how pleased she was when she found the grave stones of her McBride and Strother relatives. We saw some Nichols graves also. There was one prominent double marker with the names Willis and Mary Ann Nichols. The dates were close enough to fit date of birth of Willis W. Nichols. I took notes and a picture of the marker. Later, I found Willis W. Nichols and Mary Ann on the 1870 census of Nacogdoches County, Texas. The three children I know were the children of Willis W. Nichols and his second wife Elizabeth Clark Blakey. So I thought "that's their double grave marker I took a picture of years ago". The index to the 1880 census of Texas showed Willis Nichols in Hopkins County and not a Willis Nichols in Nacogdoches County. "Yes, he is our Willis", I thought. I looked up my cemetery notes, and found a Willis Nichols, Jr. buried at the Como Cemetery. Wanting to find out what was on the census, I got a copy of Willis Nichols and his family on the 1880 census. It did show other children besides Willis Jr. It showed Willis Nichols was born in Mississippi. His mother was born in North Carolina and wife born in Georgia. Her name was given as M. W. So, the Willis in Como Cemetery is not the father of Joseph A. B. Nichols. So what seemed to be, wasn't. Then there were those records that couldn't possibly be mine, but they were! But that's another story. What memories.

Willis W. Nichols

Willis W. Nichols and his parents were born in South Carolina. They were on the 1840 census of Bibb County, Ala. where Willis W. Nichols married twice. Both wives were named Elizabeth. The first was Elizabeth James, who died young, leaving her husband and three children. The second was Elizabeth Clark Blakey, daughter of Joseph Anthony Blakey. They were parents of seven children, one of which, was Joseph A. B. Nichols, born 1851, at Melrose, Nacogdoches County Texas. His parents were on the 1850-1860 census, but the 1870 census of Nacogdoches County shows Joseph living with his father and his third wife, Mary Ann. According to the records found on Willis W. Nichols, he was an active, knowledgeable man of apparent great strength and courage. He was a land owner, Justice of the Peace, and served in the Civil War. He was also a Texas Ranger.

Bibb Co. Ala. Pictures

William Nichols, Sr.

children

John
Elizabeth
Willis W.
William
Martha Ann
Susan
Joselin G.
William M.
Sarah Jane
Julius

William Nichols, Sr. married Jane __?__ in South Carolina.

William Nichols, Sr.

William Nichols, Sr. married a Jane, last name unknown, in South Carolina, where both were born. Their son Willis W. Nichols, (father of Joseph A. B. Nichols) was born there c1816. A son, John, may have been born there also. John was deceased and his daughter, Susan, was one of the heirs of her grandfather William Nichols, Sr. He died the 1st of January 1850 in Bibb County, Alabama. The estate of William Nichols, Sr. listed ten heirs, lands, and personal property, including a slave named Harry. Jane was to receive a widow's dower, and she filed for an allotment. The Alabama Mortality Schedule, 1850, (7th census of the US, by Marilyn Davis Hahn), list William Nichols, Sr. on page 23. He died in the month of January. The cause of death was fever, after 42 days of sickness. He was age 60, married and born in South Carolina. His occupation was Clerk of Clerk, Bibb Co. Alabama. The widow of William Nichols, Sr. is listed on page 4, no. 20 of the 1850 census of Bibb County, as Jane Nichols. It listed her at age 50, born in South Carolina. Her children were listed as Jocelin G., 20, (Registrar), William M., 22, Sarah G., 20, and Julius 12. All children were born in Alabama.

<u>William Nichols, Sr.</u>

The estate of **William Nichols (Sr.)** gives information on widow, ten heirs, (including **Willis W. Nichols**), land, a slave named Harry among his personal property, and other data. **William Nichols (Sr.)** died 1 Jan. 1850 in Bibb Co. Alabama.

From Estate records of. **William Nichols (Sr)**, Bibb Co. Ala. Courthouse, page 314 Orphans Court "A"

Leo Nichols Great, Great, Great Grandfather

<u>Julius Nichols</u>

Will 23 Jan. 1803
Proven in May 1804
Patty listed as wife

<u>children</u>

Sukey **married** Moore
Betsey **married** Cooper
Molley **married** Jones
Lucy **married** Marshall
Julius
Bobby **married** Hunt
<u>William</u>
Sally

Julius Nichols was born in Lunenburg Co. Va. and died 1804 in Abbeyville District, S. C.

Julius Nichols

Julius Nichols signed his written Will in Abbeyville District, S. C. on the 23rd of January, 1803. The Will was proven 31st of May 1804. Julius Nichols was born in Va., probably about 1725 in Lunenbourg County. He was Justice of the Peace, 1765, in Bute Co. N. C. where he was also Sheriff. His son, William Nichols, was born 1790 in S. C. and died in 1850 in Bibb Co. Alabama. This William Nichols was father of Willis W. Nichols, who was father of Joseph A. B. Nichols.

William Nichols

Will 2 June 1772
Recorded May 1774
Bute County, N.C.

children

William
Julius*
George
Margaret
Mary
Sarah
Keziah
Susannah

William Nichols, died 1774
Julius Nichols, died 1803
William Nichols, died 1850
Willis W. Nichols, died after 1874

*All had a son named Julius

The great grandfather of Joseph A. B. Nichols was Julius Nichols, born in Lunenburg Co. Va., son of William Nichols, died 1774, Bute Co. N. C. Julius Nichols had brothers William and George Nichols. Julius Nichols, his son William Nichols, and grandson Willis W. Nichols were all active as county officials. Julius Nichols was named Julius for whom, I wish I knew now. Dr. George Nicholas, first by the name Nicholas found, 1702, in Virginia, was educated in England. Related??

William Nichols, died 1774

Julius Nichols, died 1804

William Nichols, died 1850

Willis W. Nichols, died after 1874

All had a son named Julius

The name Nicholas is very ancient. "St. Nicholas" was the archbishop of Myra, was found in the 4th century. This patron saint of children and all who believed in him is known by different names with various spellings. The same applies to the Nichols family.

LUDLOW FAMILY

Sarah Ludlow was the daughter of Gabriel Ludlow, son of the immigrant from England to N. Y., c 1634, also named Gabriel Ludlow. Her father lived at Greenspring, Bruton Parish, Williamsburg, Va. He was very wealthy and a prominent man in the affairs of the colony. His daughter Sarah was the third wife of John Carter, son of the immigrant. Sarah was the mother of one child, a son, Robert, alias "King" Carter. Robert had twelve children by two wives. His first wife was Judith Armstead, and second was Betty Landon. His three daughters, Sarah, Betty, and Ludlowe, died unmarried. His other children intermarried with the Hills, Burwells, Nicholases, Churchills, Pendletons, Pages, Byrdsm Walkers, and other noted families. Sarah Ludlow Carter left many descendants who can claim the Ludlow Arms. The Nicholases may, or may not, be connected to William Nichols, father of Julius Nichols, born in Lunenburg, Co. Va. and died,1804, in Abbeville Co. S. C. We want to know the Nichols from whom our Nichols descend. Hopefully this data on the Nicholas of Virginia will not interfere with finding the ancestors of ours. More research is needed, so the real Nichols will be found.

The Times Dispatch

9 July 1907

Richmond, Virginia

Colonial Americans of Royal and Noble Descent

Alleged, Proven, and Disproved

The following data is from page 363 of the book, Colonial American of Royal and Noble Descent, by Patricia Ann Scherzinger.

1. Elizabeth Nicholas of Va.

2. Judge George Nicholas of Ky.

3. John Nicholas of Va. married Margaret Fry, the daughter of Joshua Fry

4. Capt. Lewis Valentine Nicholas of Va. (born c 1766, died 1840), married Francis Harris

5. Margaret Nicholas married Patrick Rose

6. Judge Phillip Narborne Nicholas of Va., married Mary Carter Byrd

7. Judge Robert Carter Nicholas, born 1725, and died 1788, of Williamsburg, Va.
He was a Statesman, Jurist, Patriot, and served as member of the Kings Council, treasurer of the colony and a Vestryman.

8. Wilson Cary Nicholas, born 1761 and died 1820; married 1785 to Margaret Smith

All are descendants of Sarah Ludlow. (Also of Dr. George Nicholas)

The Nicholas Family

"By request, we here give something on the Nicholas family, and though we fail to bring it in touch with the peers of England, and cannot produce an encutcheaon, yet they were so prominent in the early history of Virginia, and there are so many descendants still among us, that their record cannot be omitted among the giant sons of the old Commonwealth". This was the beginning of an article published in the Times Dispatch genealogical column, 28 Feb. 1904, Richmond, VA. It gives the name Dr. George Nicholas as being the first in Virginia, a Vestryman, 1702, in Bristol Parish. He first settled at or near Williamsburg, and had a large medical practice in the colony and in the Revolution army. He was educated in England as physician, but date of immigration is unknown. He married the widow of Mr. Burwell of Gloucester County. Dr. George Nicholas had six sons. Four were listed:

1. Robert Carter Nicholas, born in Hanover Co.

2. Colonel John Nicholas, who married Martha Fry, daughter of Colonel Joshua Fry.

3. George Nicholas, that moved to Ky.

4. Captain Lewis Valentine Nicholas.

Dear Ancestor,
Your tombstone stands among the rest;
Neglected and alone.
The name and date are chiseled out
On polished, marble stone.
It reaches out to all who care,
It is too late to mourne.
You did not know that I exist,
You died and I was born.
Yet each of us are cells of you
In flesh, in blood, in bone,
Our blood contracts and beats a pulse
Entirely not our own.
Dear Ancestor,The place you filled
one hundred years ago
Speads out amoung the ones you left
Who would have loved you so.
I wonder if you lived and loved,
I wonder if you knew,
That someday I would find this spot
And come to visit you.

Arthur: Unknown

(KVGS Journal, Fall 2201)
Courtesy of The Kanawha Valley Genealogical Society
South Charleston,WV

Joseph Anthony Blakey

Elizabeth Clark Blakey

(m.1844)
Willis W. Nichols

Susannah Stubblefield (Susan)

6. ELIZABETH CLARK BLAKEY

married 1844

WILLIS W. NICHOLS

1st Elizabeth James
children
Daniel Milton
William M.
Martha J.

children
Susan M.
Alabama D.
Fanny O. (twin)
Candis G. (twin)
Joseph A.B.
John W.
Georgia A.W.

Ancestry of

10. PENELOPE JOHNSON

+++++++++++++++++++++

wife of

CAPTAIN CHRISTOPHER CLARK

3rd Mary Ann ___
children

NICHOLS-BLAKEY-GEORGE

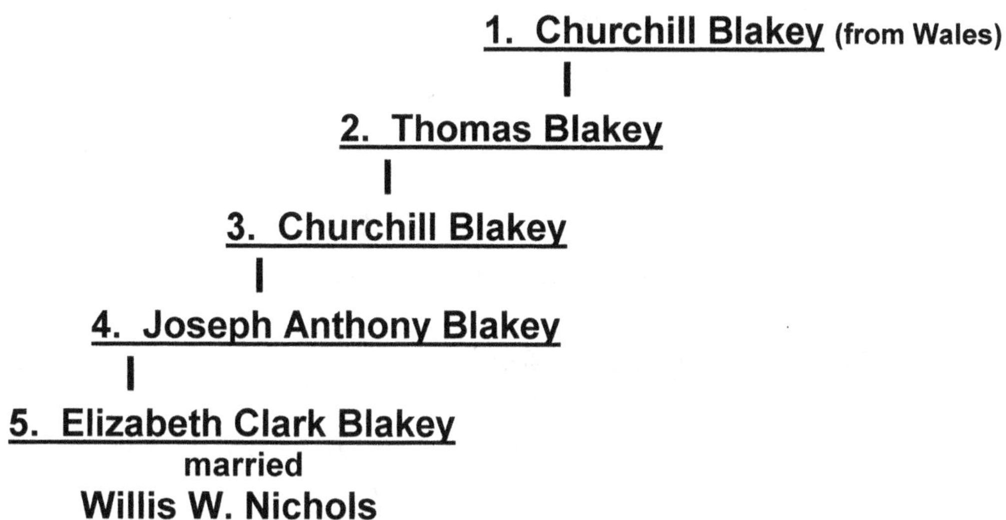

---

born in England c1580

1. Issac George

2. Henry George

3. Lt. Col. John George

4. Isaac George

5. Robert George

6. Sarah George

married

Churchill Blakey (from Wales)

BLAKEY

The following chart is for data on names found.
Any connections or order is not known.

Thomas Blakey

Walter Blakey c1450 1st British record found

Robert Blakey born 1499

Walter & Lyonell Blakey Coat of Arms

William Blakey 1st in America

1st Churchill Blakey from Wales to America
married
Sarah George

The name Blakey has been found with spelling of Blacky, Blackey, Blackely, Blacklee, Blakey and Blake.

Joseph Anthony Blakey

married

Susannah Stubblefield

March (8 or 12) 1812

children

George Washington
Joseph S.
Theodorick Stubberfield
Nancy Bethel
Fannie Oldham
Elizabeth Clark **married** Willis W. Nichols
Agnes
Mary Ann

Joseph Anthony Blakey married again to Mrs. Martha _?_ Mahan, who also had a daughter named Mary Ann.

Bibb County Probate Minutes Book H 1855-1857, page 784

Will was contested

On July 28, 1858, Martha Blakey had filed petition to probate the Will of Joseph A. Blakey, (deceased), which was contested by Fannie O [Oldham] Crow and her husband Elijah Palmer Crow, George W. Blakey, Theodorick S. Blakey, Joseph Blakey, Eliza C. Nichols, and husband Willis Nichols, Nancy B. Wood, and husband William Wood, and William M. Wilson as guardian ad litem for Agnes and Polly Blakey; who are minors and children of said Joseph A. Blakey. The Will was dated the 28th of November 1854 and John E. Sneed, a witness has departed this life. The will was upheld and cost of the contest was charged to the contestants.

From page 31 of the Alabama Records, Vol. 225 by Kathleen Jones and Pauline Jones Gandrud.

Churchill Blakey

children

Joseph Anthony **married** Elizabeth Clark
Thomas
Reuben
Churchill
Bolling
Mary
Catherine
Penelope
James
Sarah
Elizabeth

Churchill Blakey **married** Agnes Anthony 2 Aug. 1780

Churchill Blakey was a **Revolutionary War Patriot**.

Thomas Blakey

children

Sarah George
George
Thomas
Catherine
William
John
Reuben
Churchill
Joseph
Ann Haden

Thomas Blakey **married** Ann Haden 12 Jan. 1746

Churchill Blakey

children

Thomas **married** Ann Haden
Margaret
George
John
Robert
Betty
Jane
Sarah
William
Susannah
Catherine

Churchill Blakey married Sarah George
30 Nov. 1710

Anthony Haden

children

John
Ann **married** Thomas Blakey
Thomas
Ruth
William
Zachariah
Rachel
Joseph
Jane

Anthony Hayden (Haden)
married 1720
Lady Margaret Douglas

Robert George

children

Catherine
Sarah **married** Churchill Blakey
daughter
daughter
Robert
Jane
John
Richard

Robert George married Mrs. Sarah _?_ Elliot 6 July 1687

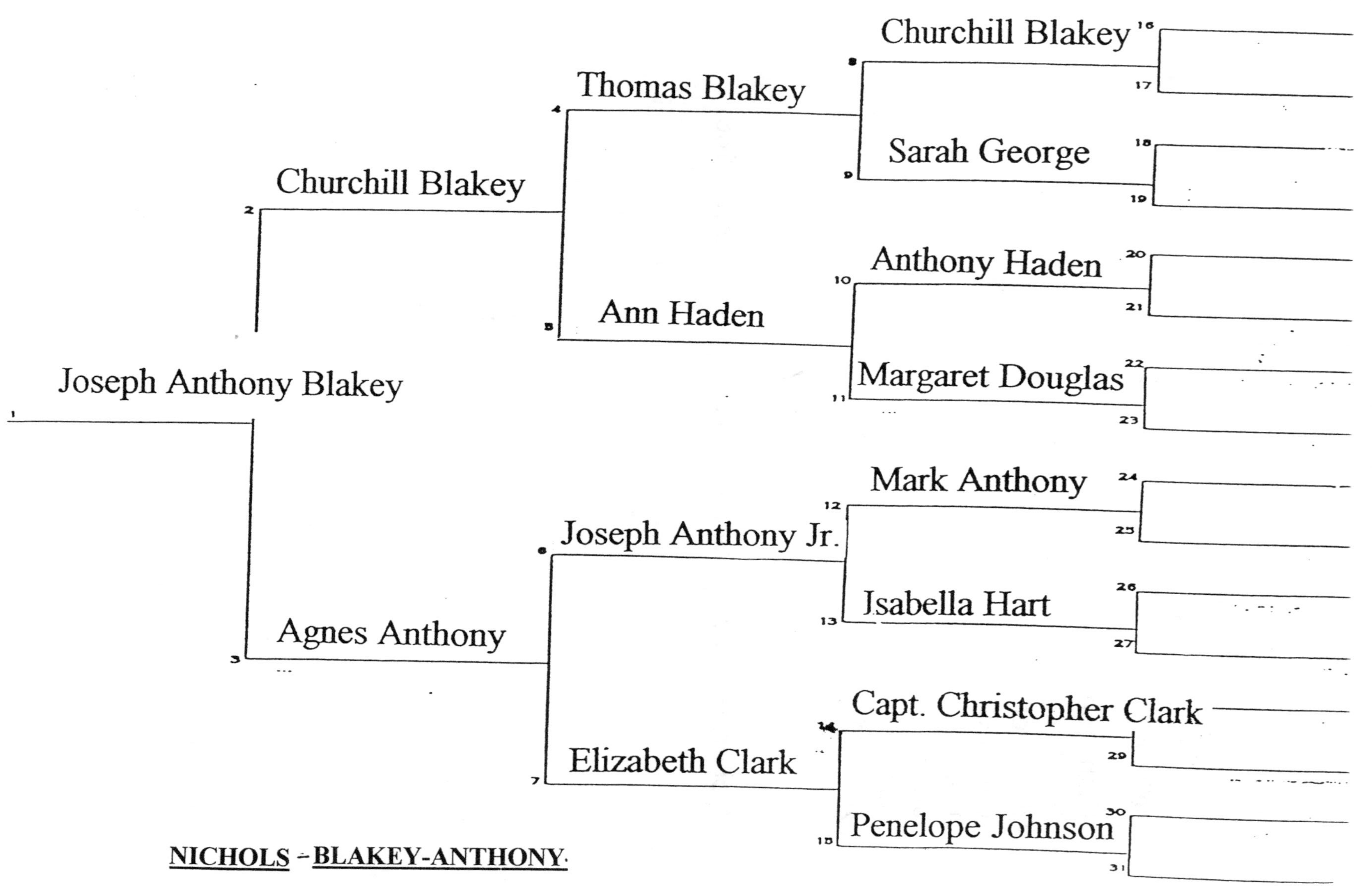

NICHOLS - BLAKEY-ANTHONY.

ANTHONY

1. Mark Anthony

|

2. Joseph Anthony

|

3. Agnes Anthony

Agnes Anthony
married 1780
Churchill Blakey

Churchill Blakey

children

Joseph Anthony
Thomas
Reuben
Churchill
Bolling
Mary
Catherine
Penelope
James
Sarah
Elizabeth

Churchill Blakey **married** Agnes Anthony 2 Aug.1780

Churchill Blakey **was a** **Revolutionary War Patriot**.

Joseph Anthony

children

Sarah
Christopher
Elizabeth
Penelope
Joseph II
James
Mary
Charles
Micajah
Agnes **married** Churchill Blakey
Rachel
Winifred
Mark
Bolling
Judith

Joseph Anthony (Sr.)
married Elizabeth Clark 27 April 1749

Joseph Anthony (Sr.) was a **Revoluntionary War Patriot**.

Mark Anthony

children
Joseph
John

Mark Anthony married **Isabella Hart**

Anthony-Hart

Mark Anthony came from Genoa, Italy to Virginia, and settled in the James River Section. According to legend, he was captured by pirates, sold into slavery in Algiers, killed his guard, and escaped to a ship bound for Virginia. He was indentured there for his passage and possessed a long genealogy showing descent from Mark Anthony and Cleopatra. This was destroyed in a bonfire by his Quaker descendants, considering it worldly vanity. Elizabeth Clark Blakey who married, 1844, Willis W. Nichols, was a great, great, granddaughter to Mark Anthony and Isabella Hart.

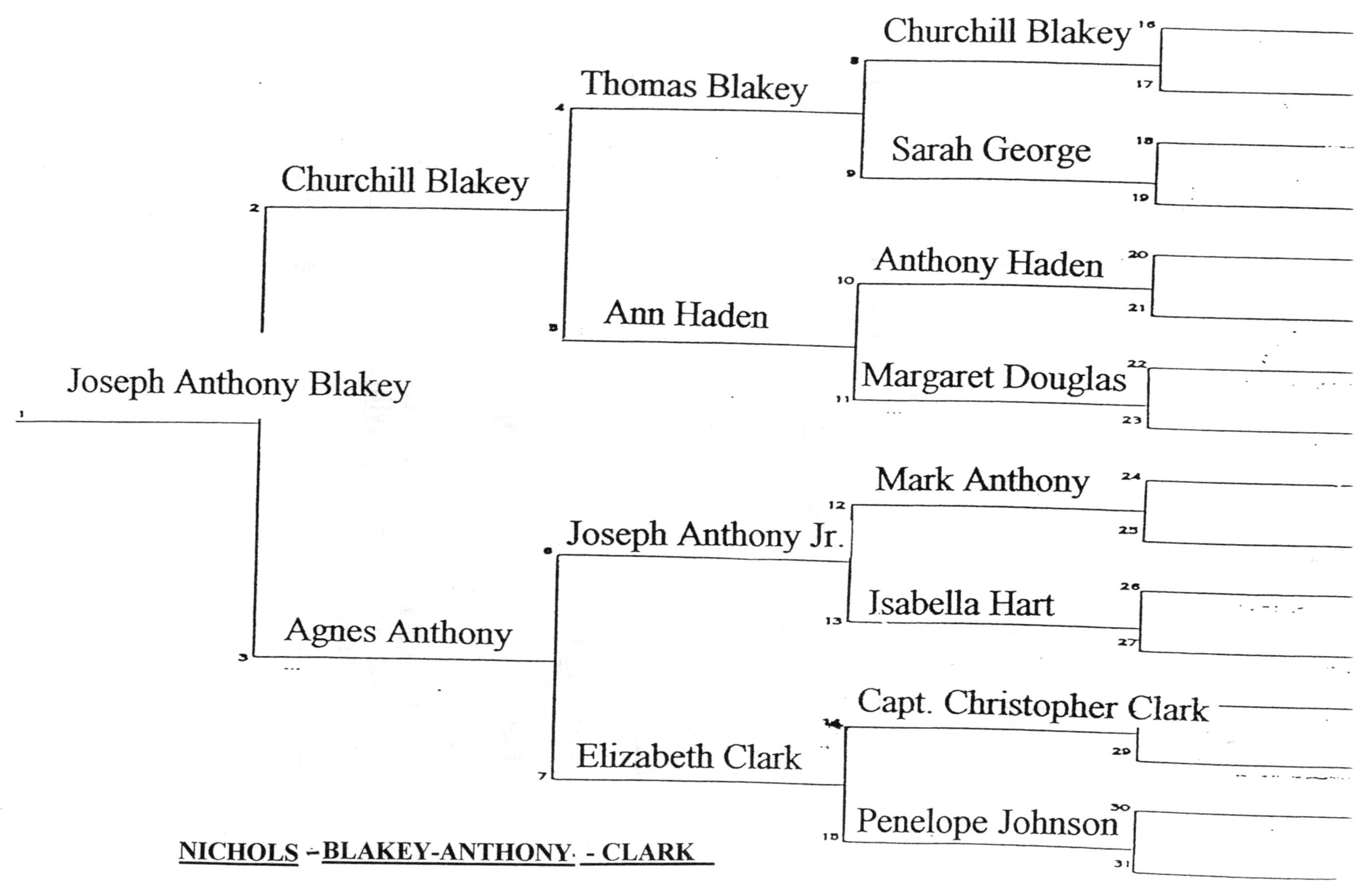

NICHOLS - BLAKEY-ANTHONY - CLARK

CLARK

gen.#

1. Michael Clark

born in England; married in England; died Aug. 5, 1678, in Barbados;
married **Margaret** , born in England; died after 1679 in Barbados

2. Micajah Clark

born in England; married by 1669 in England; died in Virginia;
married **Sally Ann Moorman** born in England; died in Virginia

3. Captain Christopher Clark

born 1681 in Nanesemond or New Kent Co. Virginia; married ca 1709 in Virginia; 1754 Louisa Co., Virginia;
married **Penelope Johnson** (Christopher and Penelope are parents of **Elizabeth Clark**)

---

1. Thomas Moorman

visited Virginia in 1619 on vessel Bona Nova

2. Captain Zachariah Moorman

born 1620 in Isle of Wright Co. in Hampshire, England; in ca 1641 in Belfast, Ireland;
married **Mary Ann Candler**; born in England; died in Barbados (her father is **Lt. William Candler**; Lt. in Cromwell's Army)

3. Sally Ann Moorman; born in England; died in Virginia

<u>Joseph Anthony</u>

<u>children</u>

Sarah
Christopher
Elizabeth
Penelope
Joseph II
James
Mary
Charles
Micajah
<u>Agnes</u> **married** Churchill Blakey
Rachel
Winifred
Mark
Bolling
Judith

Joseph Anthony (Sr.)
married Elizabeth Clark 27 April 1749

Joseph Anthony (Sr.) was a **Revoluntionary War Patriot**.

Captain Christopher Clark

children

Agnes
Rachel
Sarah
Micajah
Bowling
Elizabeth **married** **Joseph Anthony**

Captain Christopher Clark, 1709
married
Penelope Johnson

Micajah Clark

chidren

Edward
Christopher **married** **Penelope Johnson**
Francis

Micajah Clark **married** **Sallie Ann Moorman** by 1669
in England

<u>Michael Clark</u>

<u>children</u>

Francis
Edward
Roger
William
Thomas
Christopher
<u>Micajah</u> **married** Sally Ann Moorman

Michael Clark **married** Margaret _?_ in England

<u>Captain Zachariah Moorman</u>

<u>children</u>

<u>Sallie Ann</u> **married** **Micajah Clark**
Charles
Thomas

Captain Zachariah Moorman **married** Mary Ann Candler in Belfast, Ireland c 1641

CLARK-MOORMAN-CANDLER

---

1. Michael Clark

|

2. Micajah Clark

|

3. Captain Christopher Clark

married

Penelope Johnson

---

1. Thomas Moorman

|

2. Captain Zachariah Moorman

|

3. Sallie Ann Moorman

married

Micajah Clark

---

1. Lt. William Candler

|

2. Mary Ann Candler

married

Capt. Zachriah Moorman

Captain Christopher Clark was the owner of 50,000 acres of land in Hanover, Albemarle and Louisa County, Virginia. He married Penelope Johnson in 1709, served the Hanover County Militia in 1727, and was the High Sheriff in 1731. He was a Quaker, and in 1749, was overseer of a friends' meeting near Sugarloaf Mountain. It is believed by many that he was related to George Rogers Clark, conqueror of the northwest, and his younger brother William, of the Lewis and Clark Expedition to the Pacific, and first Governor of Missouri. Research suggest they were cousins, but there has not been any published records found, to date, to document any relationship.

NICHOLS - BLAKEY – STUBBLEFIELD

Ancestry of Elizabeth Clark Blakey

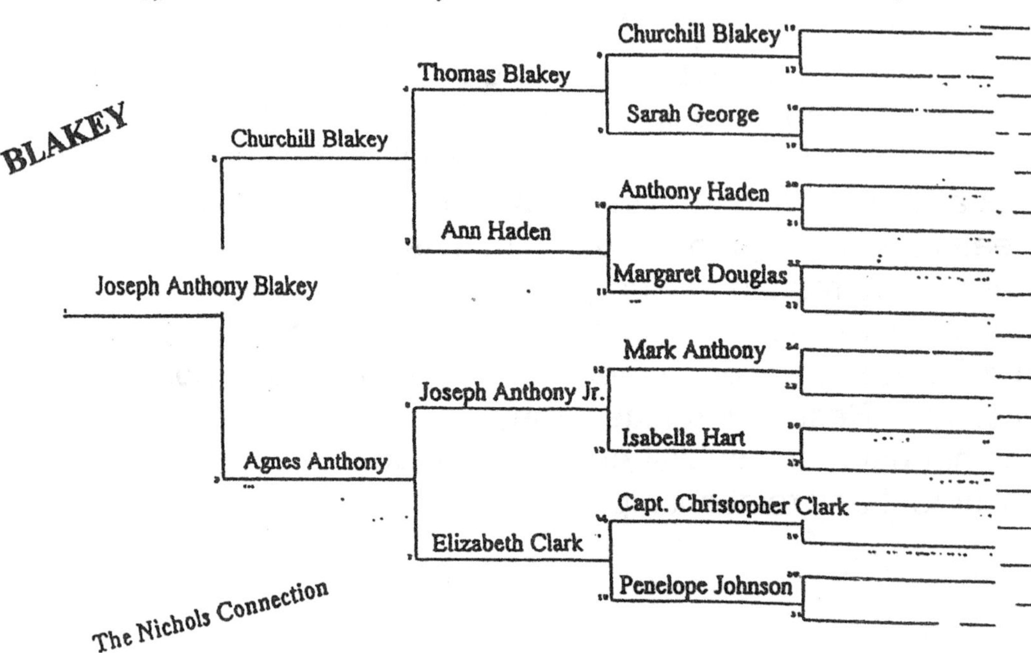

Elizabeth Clark Blakey m.1844 to Willis W. Nichols

(parents of Joseph A. B. Nichols)

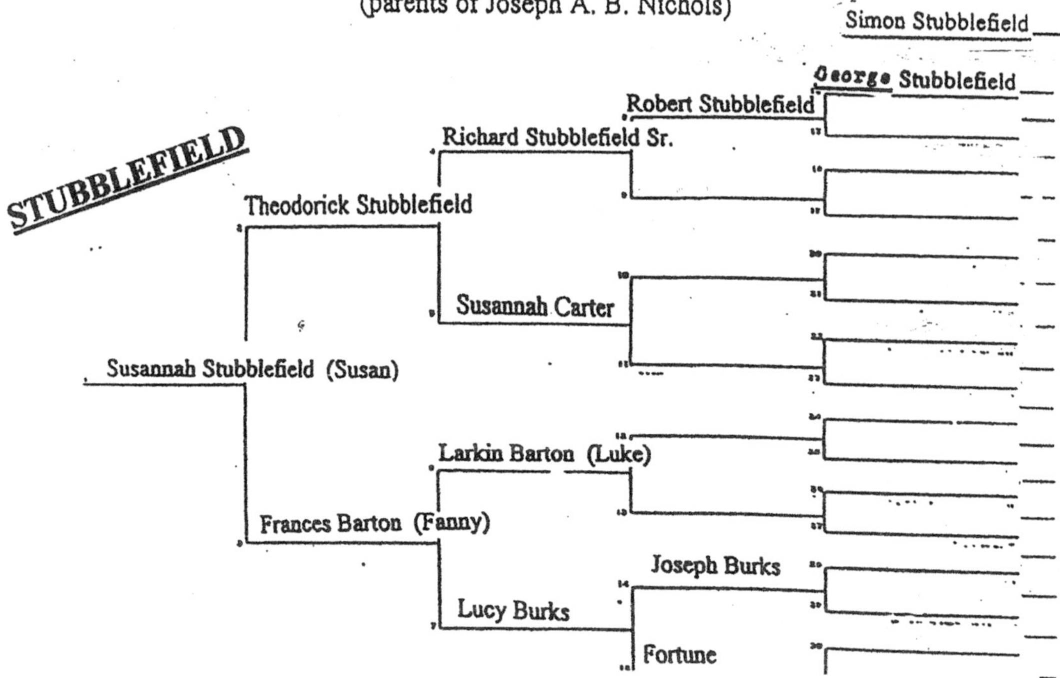

Simon Stubblefield

George Stubblefield

8 Robert Stubblefield

4 Richard Stubblefield Sr.

2 Theodorick Stubblefield

5 Susannah Carter

1 Susannah Stubblefield (Susan)

6 Larkin Barton (Luke)

3 Frances Barton (Fanny)

14 Joseph Burks

7 Lucy Burks

15 Fortune

BLAKEY - STUBBLEFIELD - BARTON - BURKS

Stubblefield-Barton-Burke-Beverly-Carter

Frances Barton was the daughter of Larkin Barton and Lucy Burks. She was known as Fanny Barton, and her father as Luke Barton. She married Theodorick Stubblefield, who died in Bibb Co. Ala. His Will was signed 30 Sept. 1821. Thomas Barton was referred to as "My Brother in-law" in his Will. Also mention was "My son-in-law" Joseph A. Blakey. Theodorick and Fanny Stubblefield were parents of Susan Stubblefield, who married Joseph Anthony Blakey. Their daughter, Elizabeth Clark Blakey married Willis W. Nichols, father of Joseph Anthony Blakey Nichols.

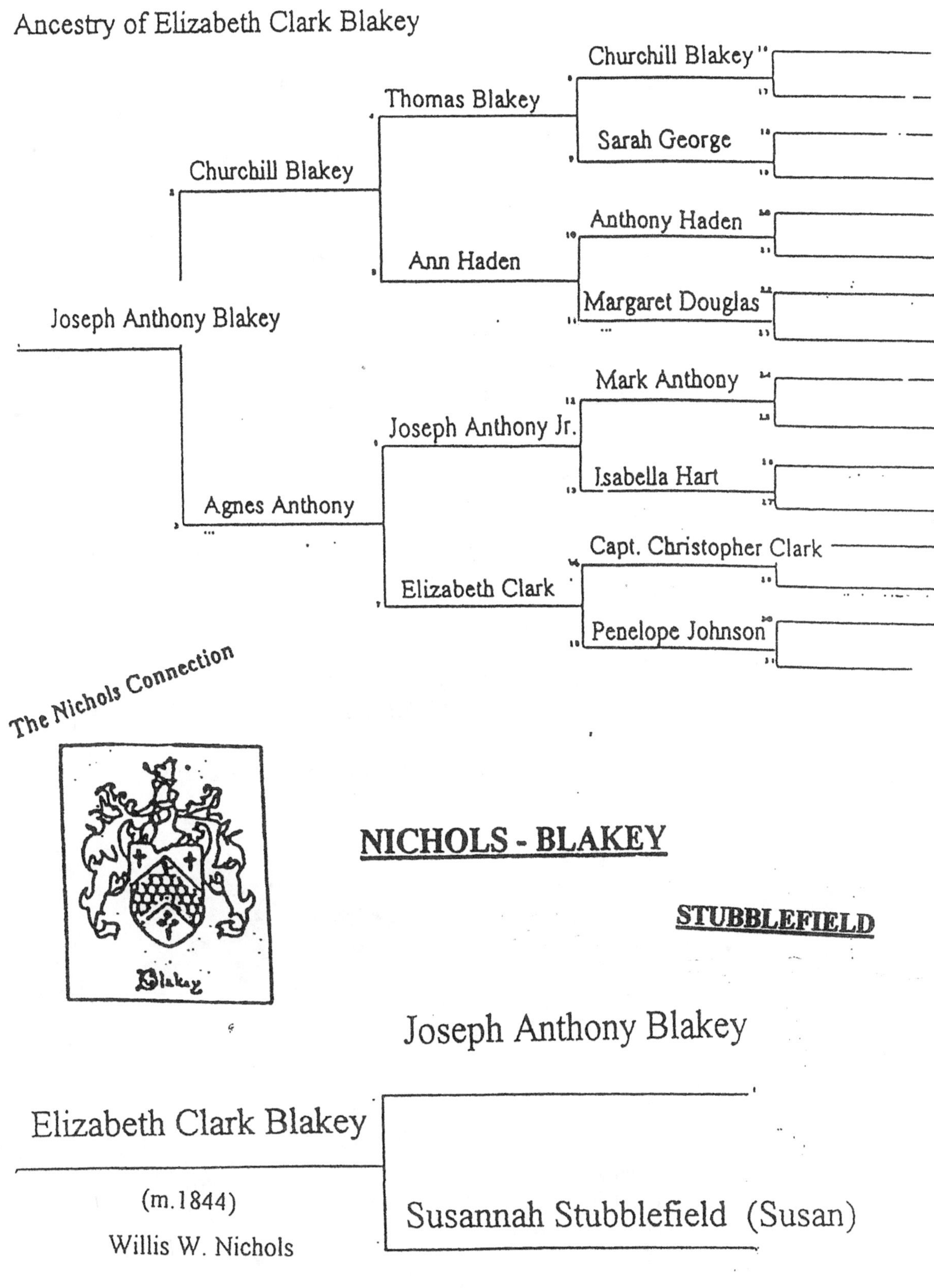

Ancestry of Elizabeth Clark Blakey
Churchill Blakey
Thomas Blakey
Sarah George
Churchill Blakey
Anthony Haden
Ann Haden
Margaret Douglas
Joseph Anthony Blakey
Mark Anthony
Joseph Anthony Jr.
Isabella Hart
Agnes Anthony
Capt. Christopher Clark
Elizabeth Clark
Penelope Johnson
The Nichols Connection
Blakey
NICHOLS - BLAKEY
STUBBLEFIELD
Joseph Anthony Blakey
Elizabeth Clark Blakey
(m.1844)
Willis W. Nichols
Susannah Stubblefield (Susan)

STUBBERFIELD

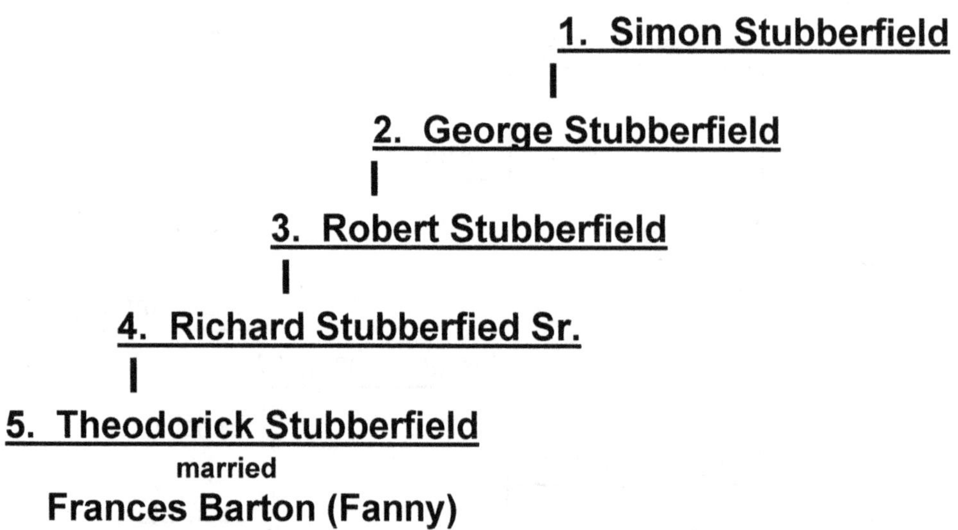

Theodorick and Frances
are Parents of Susannah Stubberfield (Susan)

Susan Stubberfield married Joseph Anthony Blakey

Joseph Anthony Blakey

married

Susannah Stubblefield

March (8 or 12) 1812

children

George Washington
Joseph S.
Theodorick Stubberfield
Nancy Bethel
Fannie Oldham
Elizabeth Clark **married** Willis W. Nichols
Agnes
Mary Ann

Joseph Anthony Blakey married again to Mrs. Martha _?_ Mahan, who also had a daughter named Mary Ann.

Theodorick Stubberfield

children

Susannah
Elizabeth

Theodorick Stubberfield **married** **Francis (Fanny) Barton**
28 March 1779 in Guilford Co. N. C.

Richard Stubblefield
Revolutionary War Patriot

children

Tilman J.
Robert C.
Beverly B.
William L.
Theodorick
Richard C.
Susanna
Martha S.
Sarah
Elizabeth

Richard Stubblefield served in the Revolutionary War as Captain. He was the great, great, grandfather of **Joseph A. B. Nichols**.

Robert Stubblefield

children

George
Thomas
Edward
Richard

Robert Stubblefield, of Culpepper Co. Va.
married Ann __?___.

George Stubblefield

children

George
Harry
Beverly
Robert
Peter

George Stubblefield **married** Catherine Beverly, **daughter of** Harry Beverly

---

Simon Stubblefield

children

Robert

Simon Stubblefield owned land in Glouster Co., Va.

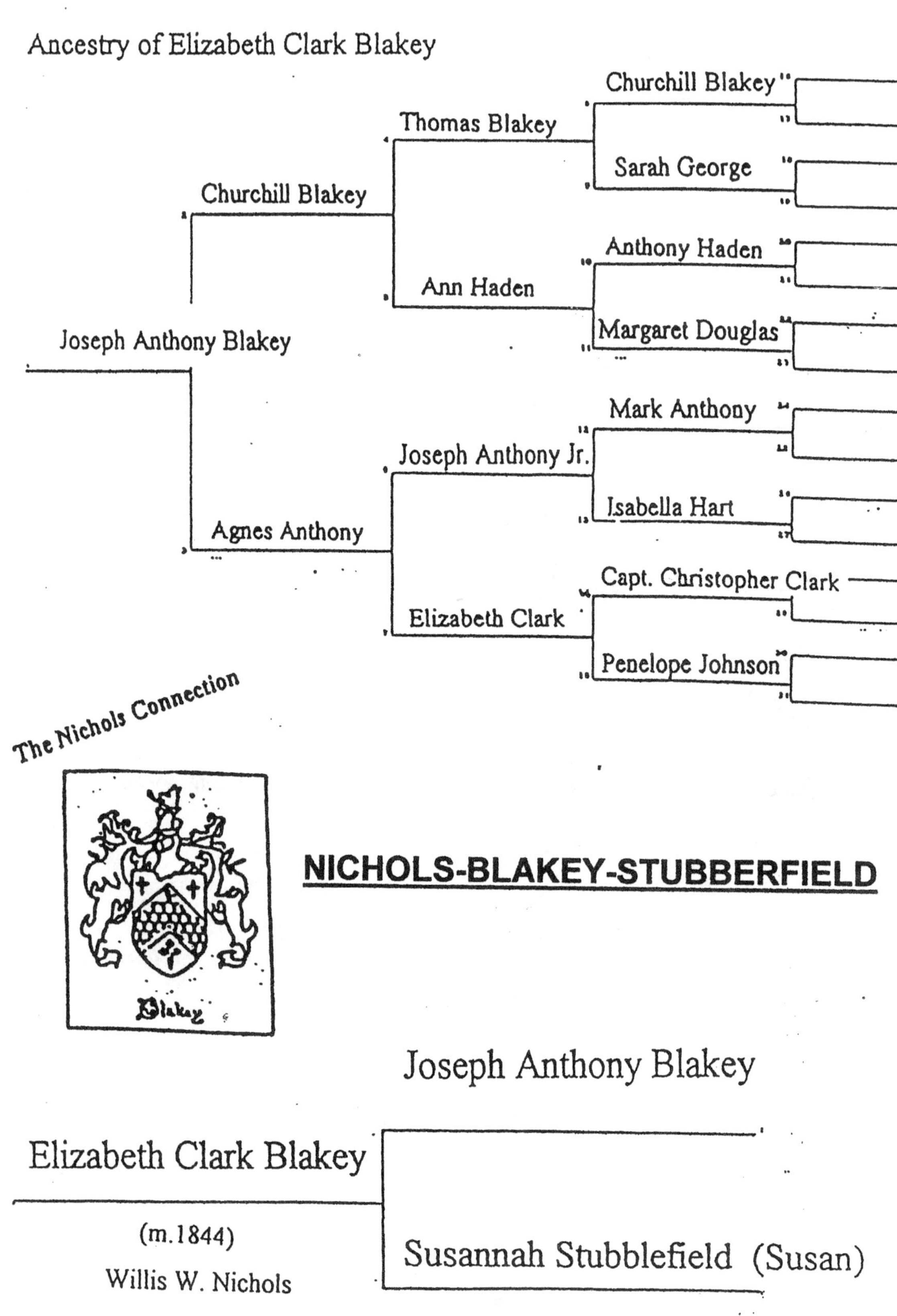

Ancestry of Elizabeth Clark Blakey
Joseph Anthony Blakey
Churchill Blakey
Agnes Anthony
Thomas Blakey
Ann Haden
Joseph Anthony Jr.
Elizabeth Clark
Churchill Blakey
Sarah George
Anthony Haden
Margaret Douglas
Mark Anthony
Isabella Hart
Capt. Christopher Clark
Penelope Johnson
The Nichols Connection
Blakey
NICHOLS-BLAKEY-STUBBERFIELD
Joseph Anthony Blakey
Elizabeth Clark Blakey
(m.1844)
Willis W. Nichols
Susannah Stubblefield (Susan)

Larkin Barton

children

Gibson
Caroline
Elizabeth Ann Matilda
Martha Washington
Fanny
Clary Fortune
Thomas

Larkin (Luke) Barton

married

Lucy Burks

Joseph Burks

Revolutionary War Patriot

children

Joseph H.
Benajah S.
William
Clary
Hudson
Frances
daughter
Betsy
John
Lucy
Nancy
Charles
Wylie P.
Sarah

Joseph Burks served in the **American Revolution.**
His wife was Fortune __?__.

Joseph Burks was a great, great, great, grandfather of **Joseph A. B. Nichols**.

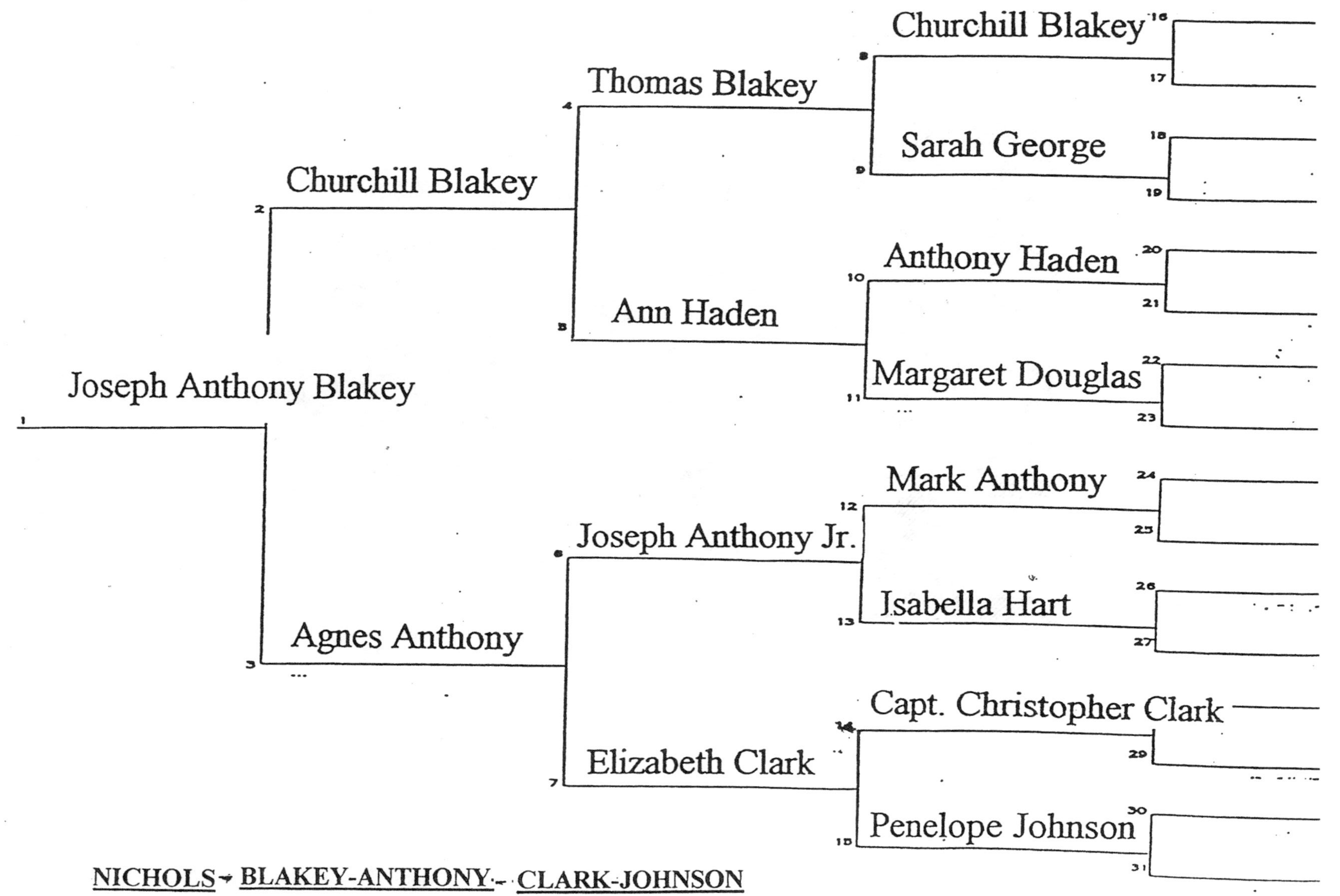

NICHOLS - BLAKEY-ANTHONY - CLARK-JOHNSON

JOHNSTON

JOHNSTON

JOHN de JOHNSTONE
1296

1550

1595

1630

CASKIEBEN

Original Caskieben 1400-1634

JOHNSTON OF THAT ILK & CASKIEBEN

1550—A BLUE SHIELD, CHARGED WITH A BEND BETWEEN A STAG'S HEAD, ERASED IN CHIEF, AND THREE CROSS CROSSLETS FITCHY IN BASE, SILVER. (AS FOUND IN THE KERR ARMORIAL, WHICH DATES ABOUT 1550) . . . .

1595—THE SEAL OF JOHN JOHNSTON OF THAT ILK, WHICH SEAL, IN RED WAX WAS ATTACHED TO "CASKIEBEN'S ACQUITTANCE OF THE PRYCE OF JOHNSTON, JUNE 7, 1595". (THREE BAGS, ONE STAG AND ONE CROSS CROSSLET)

1630—THREE STAG'S HEADS ERASED, APPEAR IN THE CHIEF IN PLACE OF THE ONE FOUND IN THE KERR ARMORIAL (SHIELD BLUE HEAD AND CROSS CROSSLETS IN SILVER) . . . .

6. ELIZABETH CLARK BLAKEY

married 1844

WILLIS W. NICHOLS

1st Elizabeth James		3rd Mary Ann ___
children	children	children
Daniel Milton	Susan M.	
William M.	Alabama D.	
Martha J.	Fanny O. (twin)	
	Candis G. (twin)	
	Joseph A.B.	
	John W.	
	Georgia A.W.	

Ancestry of

10. PENELOPE JOHNSON

++++++++++++++++++++

wife of

CAPTAIN CHRISTOPHER CLARK

10. Penelope Johnson

Penelope Johnson was a daughter of Edward Johns(t)on, immigrant, and Elizabeth Walker. She was the first of her family to be born in America. She was born 4 Aug. 1684, and was baptized 17 Nov. 1684, at St. Peters Parish, New Kent County, Virginia. Her father Edward Johnston changed the spelling of Johnston to Johnson after coming to America. He also became a Quaker. Penelope Johnson married, 1709, Captain Christopher Clark. They were both Quakers. The family of Capt. Christopher Clark referred to their Clark "cousins" in letters. It is believed by historians that George Rogers Clark, his brother William Clark (of Lewis & Clark Expedition), and family are related. The two Clark families were friends. See "Anthony Roots and Branches" by Nancy Vasti Anthony Jacob for geneology of the George Rogers Clark family, and more information on Clark.

Penelope Johnson descends from many ancient and royal lineage. She is great, great, great, grandmother of Joseph A. B. Nichols. His mother, Elizabeth Clark Blakey, 2nd wife of Willis W. Nichols is the link that ties his descendants to the ancestry of Penelope Johnson; the Nichols connection to ancient and royal families.

JOHNSTON

Thomas Johnston
I
Gilbert de Johnston
I
Adam Johnston
I
Steven de Johnston
I
John de Johnston
I
Gilbert de Johnston
I
Alexander Johnston
I
William Johnston
I
James Johnston
I
William Johnston
I
George Johnston
I
Dr. Arthur Johnston
I
Edward Johnston
I
Penelope Johnson
I
Elizabeth Johnson
I
Agnes Anthony
I
Joseph Anthony Blakey
I
Elizabeth Clark Blakey
married
Willis W. Nichols

The Leo Nichols family Connection to the charts and the Ancestry of Penelope Johnson

gen. #

10. PENELOPE JOHNSON b. 8-4-1684 VA
married CAPT. CHRISTOPHER CLARK

9. ELIZABETH CLARK b. 1722 VA
married VA JOSEPH ANTHONY SR.

8. AGNES ANTHONY b. 1761 VA d.c. 1830 GA
married 1780 CHURCHILL BLAKEY

7. JOSEPH ANTHONY BLAKEY b. 1783 VA d. 1857 ALA
married 1812 GA SUSAN STUBBLEFIELD b.c. 1785 d.c.1840 ALA

6. ELIZABETH CLARK BLAKEY b.c.1821 d.c.1865 TEX
married 1844 WILLIS W. NICHOLS ALA

5. JOSEPH A. B. NICHOLS b. 1851 TEX d. 1881-87 TEX
married 1874 LA MARTHA JANE CANNON b. 1845 TEX d. 1902 TEX

4. WILLIAM DANIEL NICHOLS (WILL) b. 1874 TEX d. 1955 LA
married 1911 LA LILLIAN COUTEE (LILLIE) b. 1888 LA d. 1957 LA

3. LEO NICHOLS b. 1929 LA
married HELEN LEE FERN BROWN b. 1930 LA

2. (Children of Leo and Helen Nichols)
Ronald Edmund Nichols
Barbara Ann Nichols
Carolyn Faye Nichols
Belinda Lenae Nichols
Leo Stephen Nichols
Daniel Norman Nichols
Janie Lucretia Nichols

1. (Grandchildren of Leo and Helen Nichols)
...a bunch of them...

10. Penelope Johnson
married c 1709
10. Capt. Christopher Clark

children

Agnes
Rachel
Sarah
Micajah
Bowling
Elizabeth **married** Joseph Anthony

Edward Johnston

children

Anthony **born** 1678
Thomas **born** 1680
Elizabeth **born** 1682
10. Penelope **born** 1684 **Penelope Johnson**
Rachel **born** 1686
Arthur
John
Michael
Rebecca **born** 1698
Benjamin **born** 1701
William **born** 1703

Edward Johnston
married
Elizabeth Walker in New Kent Co., Va.

<u>Walker</u>

John Walker
I
John Walker
I
Samuel Walker
I
Alexander Walker
I
<u>Elizabeth Walker</u>

Elizabeth Walker married, 1677, Edward Johnston at St. Peter's Parish, New Kent Co. Virginia. They were parents of Penelope Johnson, wife of Capt. Christopher Clark.

Dr. Arthur Johnston

1st wife	2nd wife
Mary Kynuncie (died 1612)	**Barbara Gordon** (died 1650)
children	**children**
James	Barbara
Ludovik	Elizabeth
Nicholes	Margaret
George	William
Mary	Edward
Susdnnah	Daniel
	(13 or more)

Dr. Arthur Johnston was a Latin Poet and Physician. He was born, 1547, at Caskieben, Scotland.
Penelope Johnson was his grand daughter.

Dr. Arthur Johnston

Dr. Arthur Johnston was the fourth great grandfather of Elizabeth Clark Blakey, who was the second wife of Willis W. Nichols. Arthur Johnston was born, 1587, at Caskieben, Aberdeenshire, Scotland. He was a Latin Poet and a physician. He was physician to King James VI of Scotland (later James I of England) and King Charles I of England. He and his second wife, Barbara Gordon, were parents of Edward Johnston, the immigrant, and father of Penelope Johnson.

Joseph A.B. Nichols was a member of the 8th generation in descent from Dr. Arthur Johnston.

Clan Johnston/e in Ameri...

Founded 1976

Reply to:
LORAND V. JOHNSON
17600 PARKLAND DRIVE
SHAKER HEIGHTS, OHIO 44120

January 2 1982

Experience Scotland '82
Conference Centre,
University of Aberdeen,
Regent Walk, Old Aberdeen

Dear Sirs:

I note in the Highlander magazine an announcement of 'Experience Scotland '82'.

The unfortunate political and religious activities of the 17th and early 18th centuries literally caused the extrusion of the numerous Johnston of Caskieben families to England and to America, much to the advantage of the later countries.

As a single instance, the Quaker merchant James Johnston, premature twin child of Sir Thomas Johnston of Craig, by his second wife Mary Irvine of Kingcausie, born January 1656, bapt. 7-20-1656. (His twin sister was Barbara, born in Jan., died March 3, and baptised posthumously July 4 1656). James married 11-23-1672 to Margaret Alexander, daughter and heiress of the Aberdeen Merchant John Alexander. Quaker merchant took his three sons, William, John and Alexander to New Kent Co. Va., and James died and was buried at 'Old-Town', Virginia. Quaker records were so exact that some 20,000 descendants of the brothers William and John are known in America. A book concerning the descendants and one concerning the ancestry of William and John Johns(t)on are in the Aberdeen Public Library.

As spokesman for Caskieben Johnstons in America, we are definately interested in 'Experience Scotland '82', and I might anticipate that some 30 persons might wish to matriculate in the course. Many of us had anticipated 1986, the centenial for the founding of Marischal College, with the arms of Sir John Johnston still on the ceiling, and oil portraits of Dr Arthur and Dr. William Johnston, his brothers.

Please send a supply of leaflets for distribution to prospective matriculants.

Sincerely,

L V Johnson

Lorand V. Johnson M.D.

Council:

Wm. H. Johnston, *President*
Maxwell Berry-Johnston, M.D., *Vice-President*
Sir Thomas A. Johnston, Bart, *Vice-President*
Coy K. Johnston, Esq., *Treasurer*
(Mrs.) Patricia A. Johnston, *Secretary, Registrar*
(Mrs.) Alvaretta K. Register, *Archivist, Genealogist*
Dr Johnstone Parr, *Historian* (Annandale)
Lorand V Johnson, M.D., *Historian* (Caskieben)
(Mrs.) Daphne Scott, *Newsletter Editor*
(Mrs.) Donald Osborne Hays, *Membership*
Lynn W. Holmes
(Mrs.) Gerald R. Fling

Clan Johnston/e in America

Founded 1976

Reply to:

LORAND V. JOHNSON
17600 PARKLAND DRIVE
SHAKER HEIGHTS, OHIO 44120

January 3, 1982

To Johns(t)on descendants
of Caskieben:

The University of Aberdeen is organizing a one week introduction to the history, culture and historic locations of Aberdeenshire, to be held the last week in August. Room and meals will be provided in one of Aberdeen University 'Halls of Residence'.

The week will consist of lectures and film presentations, plus conducted tours of the area. The last day, September 4, will be a day at the Braemar Gathering, the famous Highland Games, held near Balmoral Castle, and will be attended by the Royal Family.

A leaflet with full details is available from: EXPERIENCE SCOTLAND '82, Conference Centre, University of Aberdeen, Regent Walk, Old Aberdeen Scotland. AB9 1FX.

Probably no century has been more cruel to its people, than was the 17th century to Aberdeen. The unfortunate political, economic and religious actions literally caused the extrusion of the numerous family of 'Johnston of that Ilk, and of Caskieben'. An American audience is most fortunate to hear discussion by this eminant faculty, and in the native city.

Conducted tours could include: Dunottar Castle, where were imprisoned in a dungeon several hundred leaned Presbyterian ministers who refused to take an oath of the second episcopy; the castle of Caskieben, now called 'Keith Hall'; (which reckless, young, Sir George Johnston, 1st Bt. wadset (mortgaged) the entire estate for a pitance, and with no ability to repay); the second Caskieben, still so designated, which was seized by the English Crown following the declaration as a traitor, Sir John Johnston following the Battle of Sheriffsmuir(he avoided execution by hiding in Edinburgh, where he died [illegible]); the Quaker cemetary of Alexander Jaffray, where is buried Quakeress Barbara (daughter of William Forbes of Cragivar), mother of Elizabeth Johnston who married first Alexander Whyt, Regant Marischal College, married secondly Quaker George Keith, whose daughter Mary married George Walker of Virginia; Drum Castle, given by Robert Bruce to William de Irvine, ancestor of Mary Irvine who married as second wife, Sir Thomas of Craig; Provost Skene's House, bought by George Skene 1669, son of Alexander and Anna Johnston Skene; Castle of 7th Lord Forbes, whose daughter Christian married Sir George Johnston, who also inherited the estates of Alexander Hay, his grandfather, and of William Hay, his uncle.

MEMBER
THE COUNCIL OF SCOTTISH CLAN ASSOCIATIONS

If you anticipate any interest in the trip, please contact me immediately. If sufficient number justifies a group travel arrangement at discount fares and total baggage and tip arrangements, the itinerary should be made immediately. Lodging and meals at the University is most convenient, and organized sight-seeing for the select group should be most informative.

Sincerely,

Lorand V. Johnson M.D.

JOHN de JOHNSTONE
1296

1550

1595

1630

VIVE UT POSTEA VIVAS

CASKIEBEN

June 7 1984

Helen Nichols
POBox 146
Bethany La. 71007

Dear Mrs Nichols:

I shall attach a copy autographed to Leo & Helen Nichols. As I came here, I brought two boxes of Ancestry books, and these may be the last of the 1972 edition. I do have some that were in 1975 bound with the Crimond volume, for those who wanted the entire history of the greater family, and have about 700 pages and are $40.00.

Of the 500 that I had printed in 1942, some 50 were still left in 1972, and it seems that it took only 12 years to sell the later 500. At my age, and without secretarial help, I doubt that any more will be printed. I am told that the cost of reprinting the 1972 book would be $50. each at present prices for binding. It has been a lifetime work of joy. If I take a group to Aberdeen next year, perhaps you can go along and see the castles and land. When I printed the 1972 book, people were paying $100. for a rare copy of the 1942 book, which had the same 3 generation charts in it.

I have here 9 books for whomever requests them. I should return to Cleveland in two weeks, but my sister can mail more books if you address the letter to: Mrs Phyllis Rodenberg, 34 Nurmi Drive Ft Lauderdale Fl 33301

I do not have the Penelope Johnston Clark charts here, but shall send some from Cleveland later.

I presume either address?? Shreveport or Bethany?

Sincerely, LVJ.

·ANIMO·NON·ASTUTIA·
Gordon

Gordon

The name Gordon is as ancient as any European monarchies. Caesar gives great praise for the bravery of the people called Gordonuni in his commentaries. The original name may have come from Gordonia, a city in Macedonia. The first of the name Gordon in Scotland was Sir Adam de Gordon or Gordoun who was killed, 1093, in battle. This knight was in great favor of King Malcolm, and received many lands as rewards for his valor and merit. The Gordon Coat of Arms, pictured, is the oldest Gordon Coat of Arms in existence. The Gordons of Huntly etc., descendants of the same British Gentile Gordons, continue to have at least one boars-head on their Coat of Arms, for identity and in memory of Sir Adam Gordon I. King Malcolm had him to carry in his banner three boars-heads, or, in a field of Azure. This was to transmit to posterity the memory ot the remarkable action of Sir Adam Gordon I. He had killed a fierce boar that wasted much of the country near the woods of Huntly. The lands bestowed upon him continued to belong to Gordon families for 500 years or more. The Coat of Arms Motto, Animo non Astutia, translated means "By courage, not by stratagem."

Barbara Gordon was the second wife of Dr. Arthur Johnston. Her parents were Sir John Gordon, of Newton and Margaret Udny. She was a descendant of Sir Adam de Gordon or Gordoun, who was killed in battle in 1093 A. D. Her ancestor, Patrick de Udny, who died before 1406 was of the family that possessed the Barony of Udny since the 13th century. Barbara Gordon Johnston is the mother of Edward Johnston, who married Elizabeth Walker in Virgina. Their daughter, Penelope Johnston, married Captain Christopher Clark.

GORDON

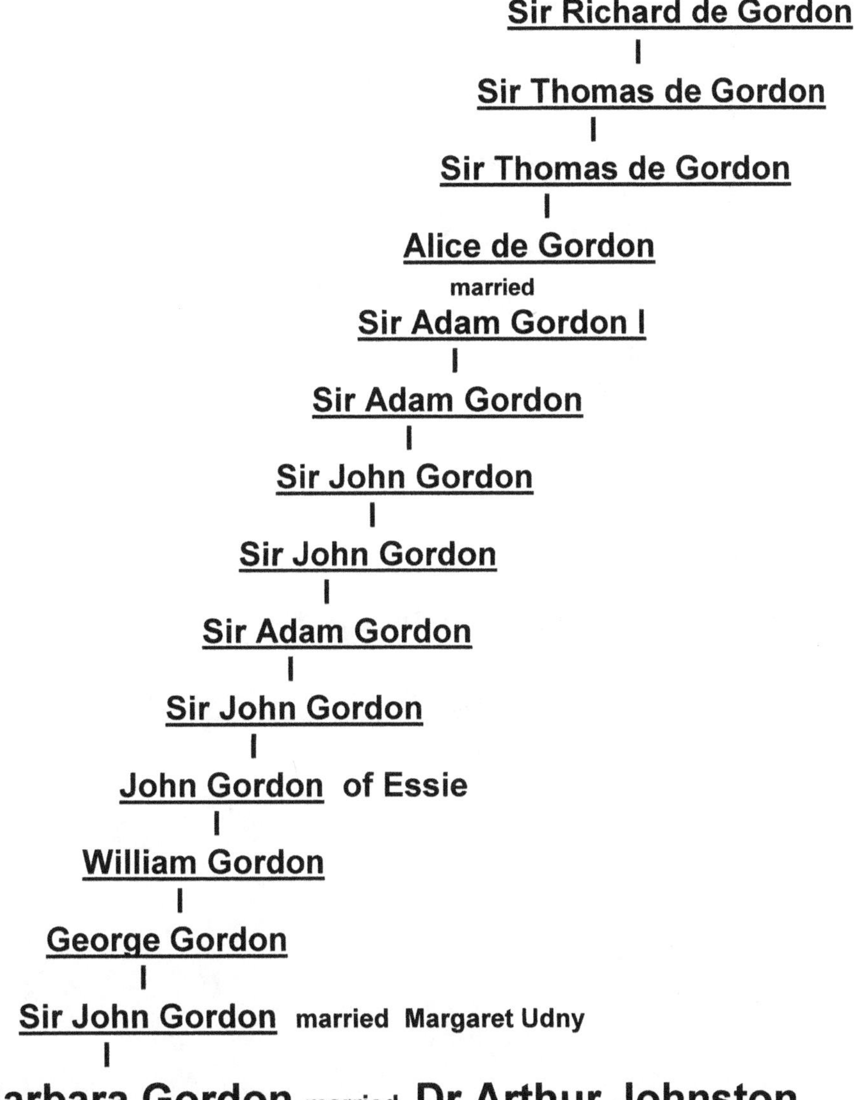
Sir Richard de Gordon
Sir Thomas de Gordon
Sir Thomas de Gordon
Alice de Gordon
married
Sir Adam Gordon I
Sir Adam Gordon
Sir John Gordon
Sir John Gordon
Sir Adam Gordon
Sir John Gordon
John Gordon of Essie
William Gordon
George Gordon
Sir John Gordon married Margaret Udny
Barbara Gordon married Dr Arthur Johnston

UDNY

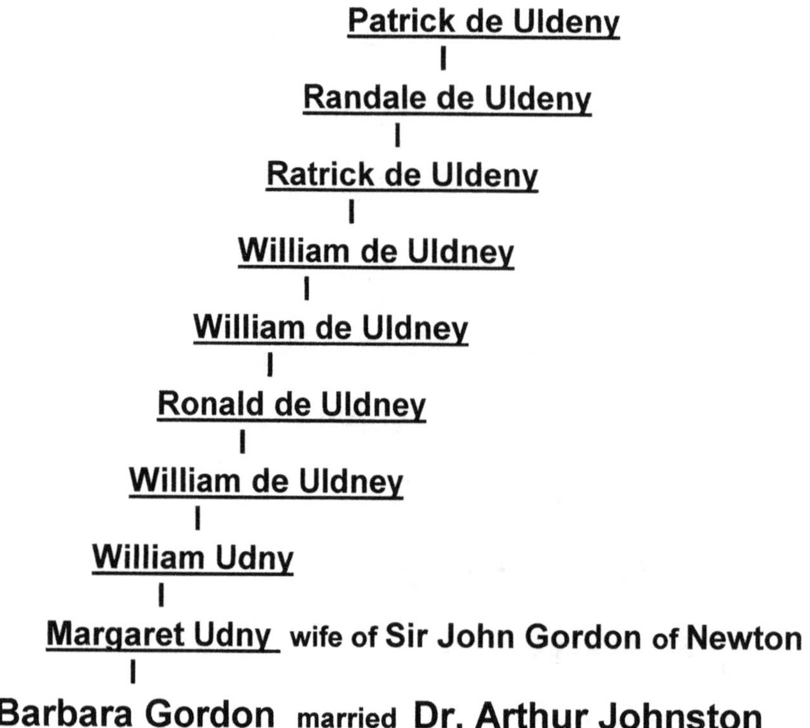

Barbara Gordon married **Dr. Arthur Johnston**

The numbers before the names on the charts are generation numbers. These charts and supplements are to be used in connections to the ***Ancestry of Penelope Johnson, and Ancestry of William and John Johnson, and Johnston of Caskieben, Crimnond and Caisemill.*** The author of both books is *Dr. Lorand Victor Johnson*, as authority on Johnson and Scottish history. He is a direct descendant of Sir John Johnston, brother of Dr. Arthur Johnston. Edward Johnson, the Immigrant, is son of 12. Dr.Arthur Johnston, and father of 10. Penelope Johnson. Penelope Johnson was born in Virginia, and wife of 10. Captain Christopher Clark.

The second wife of Willis W. Nichols, **6. Elizabeth Clark Blakey Nichols**, is the **Nichols Connection** to the ***Ancestry of Penelope Johnson***.

King of England

20. EDWARD III King of England married PHILLIPA, dau
William, Count of Hainault

19. JOHN of Gaunt married KATHERINE , mistress

18. JOHN BEAUFORT married Lady MARGARET HOLLAND

17. JOAN BEAUFORT married Sir JAMES STUART of Lorne

Sir JOHN STUART married Lady MARGARET DOUGLAS
Earl of Athol

16. ELIZABETH STUART married ANDREW, II Lord Gray

15. Lady JANET GRAY married Sir WILLIAM KEITH

14. WILLIAM, VII Lord Forbes married ELIZABETH KEITH

13. CHRISTIAN FORBES married Sir GEORGE JOHNSTON
8th of that ILK

12. Dr. ARTHUR JOHNSTON married BARBARA GORDON

11. EDWARD JOHNS(T)ON married ELIZABETH WALKER
Immigrant

10. PENELOPE JOHNSON

6. ELIZABETH CLARK BLAKEY
married
WILLIS W. NICHOLS

King of Scotland

23. Robert I, The Bruce, married Lady Isabel of Mar
King of Scotland

22. Majory Bruce married Walter, The Steward of Scotland

21. Robert II, married Elizabeth Mure, his mistress
1st King of the house of Stuart

20. John Stuart married Annabella Drumond
succeeded as Robert III, King of Scotland

19. Princess Mary Stuart married George Douglas , Earl of Angus

18. Elizabeth Douglas married Alexander, I Lord Forbes

17. James, II Lord Forbes married Egida Keith

16. William, III Lord of Forbes married Christian Gordon

15. John, VI Lord Forbes married Christian Lundin

14. William, VII Lord Forbes married Elizabeth Keith

13. Christian Forbes married Sir George Johnston
8th of that ILK

12. Dr. Arthur Johnston married Barbara Gordon

11. Edward Johns(t)on married Elizabeth Walker
immigrant

10. PENELOPE JOHNSON

6. ELIZABETH CLARK BLAKEY
married
WILLIS W. NICHOLS

32. Richard de Clare

32. Richard Fitz Gilbert, died c 1035, Founder of the House of Clare in England. Became known as Richard de Clare.

31. Gilbert de Tonebruge de Clare, 2nd Earl of Clare

30. Richard Fitz Gilbert de Clare

29. Sir Roger de Clare, 5th Earl of Clare
"The Good Earl of Hartford".

28. Sir Richard de Clare, 4th Earl of Hartford, and
6th Earl of Clare. A Surety.

27. Sir Gilbert de Clare, 5th Earl of Hartford and
Lord Glouchester. A Surety.
married **27. Isabel Marshall**, daughter of
28. William Marshall, 1st
Earl of Pembroke.

26. Isabel Clare, born 1226, married, 1240,
26. Robert Bruce, died 1295.

|

(**23. King Robert Bruce**, of Scotland
(Robert the Bruce), was a great grandson.)

The Sureties for the Observance of the Magna Charta

There are eighteen names, of the twenty five Sureties, who are lineal ancestors of the founders of the **Order of Runnemede**, and who left descendants.

On line five,
[28.] **Gilbert de Clare, Earl of Hartford and Gloucester, d. 1229.**

On line six,
[27.] **Richard de Clare, Earl of Hartford and Gloucester, d. 1262.**

Magna Charta

(Generation 3. Leo Nichols to 28. Sir Richard de Clare)

3. Leo Nichols, a great grandson of Elizabeth Clark Blakey

4. The grandchildren of Elizabeth Clark Blakey Nichols

5. The children of Elizabeth Clark Blakey Nichols

6. Elizabeth Clark Blakey
married 1844
Willis W. Nichols

7. Joseph Anthony Blakey

8. Agnes Anthony

9. Elizabeth Clark

10. Penelope Johnston

11. Edward Johnston, **Immigrant**
married
11. Elizabeth Walker

12. Dr. Arthur Johnston
married 2nd
12. Barbara Gordon

13. Christian Forbes
married
13. George Johnston, **8th of that ILK**

14. William, **7th Lord Forbes**

15. John, **6th Lord Forbes**

16. William, **3rd Lord Forbes**

17. James, **2nd Lord Forbes**

18. Elizabeth Douglas

19. Princess Mary Stewart

20. John Stewart

21. King Robert II

22. Margaret Bruce

23. **King Robert Bruce**
(Robert the Bruce) of Scotland

24. Christian Bruce

25. Robert Bruce, **Earl of Carrick**

26. Isabel Clare
born 11-2-1226
married 1240
26. Robert Bruce

27. Sir Gilbert de Clare, (a Surety of Magna Charta)
5th Earl of Hertford and Lord Glouchester, died 1217
married
27. Isabel Marshall

28. Sir Richard de Clare, (a Surety of Magna Charta)
4th Earl of Hertford and 6th Earl of Clare, died 12-30-1218
married
28. Lady Amicia Meullent

King John

(Magna Charta Grant)

25. Henry II, (1136-1167)
20th King of England
married 25. Eleanor of Aquintain.

24. King John, (1199-1216)
22nd King of England, granted the Magna Charta in 1215. This Magna Charta, or "Great Charter", became a cornerstone of modern English law. He married 24. Isabel de Talif.

23. Henry III, (1207-1272)
23rd King of England 1216,
married 23. Eleanor of Provens.

22. Edward I, **24th English King 1272,**
married Eleanor of Castile.

21. Edward II, **born 1284**
25th English King 1307
murdered in Berkley Castle.

Charlemagne

"Emperor of the West"

(Generation 26. Isabet Clare to 44. Charlemagne)

44. Charlemagne, 742-814,
married 2nd Hildegarde of Sublaib

43. Louis I, le Debonaire, **Roman Emperor**

42. Louis, of Germany

41. Carislan, **died** 880

40. Arnulph

39. Edith, of Germany

38. Henry I, **The Fowler**

37. Hedwige, **married** Hugh, **Duke of France**

36. Hugh Capet, **King of France**

35. Robert, **The Pious**

34. Henry I, **King of France**

33. Hugh Magnus

32. Isabel Vermandois,
married 1st Robert de Bellomont

31. Robert de Bellomont

30. Robert de Bellomont

29. Lady Mabel de Bellomont
married
William Meullent

28. Lady Amicia Meullant
married
28. Sir Richard de Clare, a Surety

27. Sir Gilbert de Clare, a Surety

26. **Isabel Clare**, **married** 1240,
26. **Robert Bruce**

22. Margaret Bruce

12. Dr. Arthur Johnston,
married 2nd Barbara Gordon

11. Edward Johnston, Immigrant

10. Penelope Johnson

6. Elizabeth Clark Blakey,
married 1844
Willis W. Nichols

More on de Clare and Connections

28. Sir Richard de Clare, a Surety
27. Sir Gilbert de Clare, a Surety
26. Isabel Clare, wife of 26. Robert Bruce
to Generation 44. Chalemagne
to Generation 76. Mark Anthony, 83 B.C.-30 A.D.
77. Anthony the Creton
78. Anthony, the Orator
to 69. Clodimir IV, King of the Franks died 166 A.D.
70. Marcomir IV, died 149 A.D.,
King of Franconia, married daughter of
70. Alhildis, (a descendant of 78. Anthony, the Orator.)
to 122. Priamos, King of Troy
to 138. Isaac 1946-1726 B.C.
to 149 Noah 2948-1998 B.C.
to 158 Adam 4000-3070 B.C.

Another de Clare of interest is Margaret de Clare (died 1342) married 2nd 1317 Hugh de Audley, died 1347, 6th Earl of Glouchester; Ambassador 1341 to France.

Margaret de Clare is daughter of Joan Plantageniet who married Gilbert de Clare, Knight, 9th Earl of Clare, Earl of Hertford and Glouchester. Margaret is descendant of Alfreida daughter fo Alfred to Great, King of England. Also descendant of Chalemagne.

Descendants help needed.

Our great, great, grandchildren number 11 generation in descent from William Nichols (died 1774 in N. C). We are so proud of our large family. The number of our children is seven. The number of our grandchildren, great grandchildren, and great, great, grandchildren continue to grow, and like history, is an on-going thing. Hopefully, our many descendants, for generations to come, will have the opportunity to read and know about their heritage. The help of our children and our grandchildren is needed. We encourage and appreciate their recording their own family histories making this possible.

"....but those *memories* we have will be gone all too soon, leaving this world at the same time we do, just as the m*emories* of our grandfathers and great grandmothers left with them. And unless they are given and past on, it is as if those things have never been...."

Author Unknown

(from Connie Draper)

Reference

LEO NICHOLS

State of Louisiana Birth Records Dept. of Vital Records, Baton Rouge, Louisiana Grant parish Courthouse, Colfax, Louisiana

WILLIAM "WILL"DANIEL NICHOLS

U.S. Federal Census 1880, Nacogdoches County, Texas
Letter of Mrs. Faye Agerton
U.S. Federal Census 1900 and 1910, Natchitoches Parish, La.
U.S. Federal Census 1910, Rapides Parish, Lousiana
Rapides Parish Courthouse Records, Alexandria, Louisiana
Natchitoches Parish Courthouse Records, Natchitoches , La.
Department of Vital Records, State of Louisiana Death Records, Baton Rouge, Louisiana

JOSEPH A.B. NICHOLS

U.S. Census 1860, 1880, Nacogdoches County, Texas
Sabine Parish Courthouse Records, Many, Louisiana
Rapides Parish Courthouse Records, Alexandra, Louisiana
Angelina County, Texas Courthouse Records, Lufkin, Texas
U.S. Census 1850 and 1860, Sabine Parish, Lousiana

WILLIS W. NICHOLS

Bibb County Courthouse Records, Centreville, Alabama
U.S. Federal Census 1840, Bibb County, Alabama
U.S. Federal Census 1850, 1860, and 1870, Nacogdoches County, Texas
Nacogdoches County Courthouse Records, Nacogdoches, Texas
Sabine Parish Courthouse Records, Many, Louisiana
Texas State Archives, Austin, Texas

WILLIAM NICHOLS, SR.

Bibb County Courthouse Records, Centreville, Alabama
Alabama Mortality Schueld, 1850 by Marilyn Davis Hahn, p. 23

JULIUS NICHOLS

Abbeville County Courthouse Records, Abbeyville, South Carolina
Will of Julius Nichols, Inventory of Estate

WILLIAM NICHOLS (D. 1774)

Wills, Bute County, North Carolina

THE NICHOLAS OF VIRGINIA

The Times Dispatch, Richmond, Virginia

Alabama Records, Vol. 160 by Katherine Paul Jones and Pauline Jones Gandrud, pp.21, 39, 53-57

Alabama Records, Vol. 166 by Katherine Paul Jones and Pauline Jones Gandrud, pp. 46-50

Marriage Records of Bibb County Alabama, 1820-1860 by Pauline Jones Gandrud in 1969, pp 84

Cumberland Parish, Lunnenburg County, VA 1714-1816 Vestry Book, by Landon C. Bell, p. 306

Bute County Records Book 2, 1774-1779, Will Book 2, Warren County Records, North Carolina

"The Days That Lie Behind Us," by T. Russell Shelton, The Times Dispatch, Richmond, Virginia, January 11, 1914

"Dear Ancestor" courtesy of The Kanawha Valley Genealogical Society

"The Genealogical Column," The Times Dispatch, Richmond, Virginia following dates: February 28, 1904, May 1, 1904, December 27, 1906, March 24, 1907, June 9, 1907, January 11, 1914

The Ancestry of William and John Johnson, by Lorand V. Johnson, M.D.

Johnston of Caskieben, Crimond, and Cayesmill, by Lorand V. Johnson, M.D. 1975

A Blakey Book,k 1686-1977, by Bernard Buckner Blakey, November 1977, pp. 1-15, 26-33, 57, 104

Anthony Roots and Branches, Vol. 1 by Nancy Vashti Anthony Jacob, 1983, pp. 3-6, 25-26, 303-305, 310, 534

Historic Cotile, by Patsy K. Barber, Baptist Message Press, 1966

The History of Rockingham County by Rockingham County Historical Society, pp. 177, 609

Early Families of the N. C. Counties of Rockingham and Stokes, by Jane Hunter Chapter N. S. D. A. R., p. 117

Early Georgia Wills, Settlements of Estates of Wilkes County, by Susan Quinn Smith, pp. 13, 33

The Western Heritage Sixth Edition by Donald Kagan, Steven Ozment, Frank M. Turner, Prentice Hall Publishers, Simon and Schuster, 1998, pp. 258-260

Correspondence with Mrs. S. F. Webster, member of N. S. D. A. R. on September 23, 1985, Madison, North Carolina

Interview with Dr. Lorand V. Johnson

Interviews with Nancy Vashti Anthony Jacob and her sister, Florence Anthony

Interview with Mr. B. B. Blakey

Interview with Mr. James T. McConnel, a member of the National Society Sons of the American Revolution

Interview with Susan Christine Nichols Fisher, Vidor, Texas

Interview with Connie Draper

Interview with David Vance Muckleroy, Nacogdoches, Texas

Smith, Frank M., The Lives and Times of Our English Ancestors, Logan: The Everton Publishers, 1969. Pages: 46-47, 52-53,68-69, XIV-XX

Adam, Frank, The Clans Septs, and Regiments of the Scottish Highlands 8th Edition, Johnson and Bacon Stirling. Pages 4-51. ISBN Number: 0 719 4500 6

Dobson, David, The Original Scots Colonists of Early America 1612-1783
Library of Congress Number 88-83174

Buck, J. Orton, Beard, Timothy Field, Cabaniss, Allen, Pedigrees of Some of the Emperor Charlemagne Descendants Volume III, Baltimore: 1988. Pages: 6-10, 18-23, 42-49, 60-67, XXVI-XXX. Library of Congress Number 87-39170

Smallwood, Marilyn Burch, Related Royal Families, Gainesville: Storterville, 1966. Pages: 1-15, 102-103

Steinberg, S. H., Historical Tables 58 BC-1985, New York: Garland Publishing, 1964. Pages 238-257. Library of Congress 86-18326

*In Memory of *Gloria*

The last cemetery I went to was the Forest Park Cemetery in Shreveport, Louisiana. The graveside service was for someone very dear to me. The coffin remained closed. There were many loved ones present. "We're going to miss her Helen, but we have enough memories to talk about for years." Tears flowing, and overcome with grief, this was said to comfort me by one who knows the bond her mother and I have had for a lifetime. "We'll have to remember her like the way she was living," her surviving husband told me. I asked if I could take pictures. Another daughter answered, "Yes, I'll stay with you." She, too, understood. Yes, it was the funeral of my best friend Gloria. We must have known each other in Heaven before we came to earth, we had spoken, and agreed. Our closeness was more than could be explained any other way. She died suddenly. She was buried near loved ones on earth. She is with many loved ones in Heaven now. I remember how my mother and Gloria laughed, and talked. They are together now.

Yes, I remember, I'll always remember you Gloria.

*Gloria Dell Parker Iglesias

NOTES

www.ingramcontent.com/pod-product-compliance
Lightning Source LLC
Chambersburg PA
CBHW080424270326
41929CB00018B/3153

* 9 7 8 0 7 8 8 4 3 3 6 4 1 *